Baby and Toddler Learning Fun

My very best wishes,

Sally Goldberg, Ph.D.

Baby and Toddler Learning Fun

Fifty Interactive and Developmental Activities to Enjoy with Your Child

SALLY R. GOLDBERG, PH.D.

Professor of Early Childhood Education,
Graduate Teacher Education Program,
Nova Southeastern University

PERSEUS
PUBLISHING

An earlier version of this book was published in 1981 as *Teaching with Toys*.

Cataloging-in-Publication data for this book is available from the Library of Congress.

ISBN 1–55561–310–1
Perseus Publishing is a member of the Perseus Books Group.
Find us on the World Wide Web at http://www.perseuspublishing.com

Perseus Publishing books are available at special discounts for bulk purchases in the U.S. by corporations, institutions, and other organizations. For more information, please contact the Special Markets Department at the Perseus Books Group, 11 Cambridge Center, Cambridge, MA 02142, or call (617) 252–5298.

Text design by *Brent Wilcox*
Set in 12-point Goudy by Perseus Publishing Services

First printing, October 2001
2 3 4 5 6 7 8 9 10—03 02

To Cynthia and Deborah,
who grew up with fond memories of early play.

To Cindy Randall,
a woman of many talents, beautiful inside and out.
She took it upon herself to make sure that
this book would become a reality.

Acknowledgments

I owe this book to the many parents who have used this "learn as you play" concept and loved every single one of the toys described in it. They taught me that the information in the book was invaluable and should be expanded. I also owe this second edition to the many new parents who have asked for this revised copy. They taught me that the ideas have stood the test of time and must be made available for continued use. I especially thank my family for all their input and joy. My two daughters, Cynthia and Deborah, played with the toys. My mother, Sylvia, values creativity, and I am sure it was she who instilled in me the idea for using old materials in new and constructive ways. My friend Maria Elena Buria has special energy, intuition, and spirit that inspired me to bring this book out in its new and improved form. Thank you, Maria Elena. Special thanks go to the Rascoe family. Besides their unending support, they played an active role as well. Bill and Carol helped me to photograph all the toys that are drawn in this book. They also helped me to photograph their beautiful granddaughter Cara Rascoe. She and her mom Amy posed for a few of the drawings. Marnie Cochran, Senior Editor, and Fred Francis, Project Editor, added their magic to the book and made it come alive. Thank you both for your wonderful input.

Contents

Part Three: The Endless Learning Process

Preface

From the time I discovered Lois Lenski through her beautiful children's books in the White Plains Public Library in 1954, I knew I wanted to write for children. As I went through school, I could see over and over how effective a good teaching tool was. By the time I entered Cornell University in 1965, I was ready to major in child development and minor in communication arts. These two interests led me to the study of designing teaching materials for children.

While pursuing a master's degree in educational curriculum and instruction, I knew I wanted to work in the field of educational materials development. However, the advice came from all around, "You must be a teacher before you can design a product for other teachers. That is the only way you will understand their wants and needs." I took that advice and chose to teach first grade. I chose first grade because in 1971 that level was considered the beginning of academic learning. I wanted to be the one to give children a good start in school. I found excellent materials available in the schools where I taught, but often when I had to present a particular topic, such as teaching a particular reading skill or demonstrating a particular mathematical principle, I needed to make my own teaching materials.

After four years of teaching, I had developed many games, toys, and books for use in the classroom. Themes of "familiarity," "repetition," and "begin at the beginning" ran through my work. When my older daughter was born in 1976, I intended to stop teaching temporarily and begin to market some of the educational materials I had developed. I did stop teaching, but before I could begin other projects, I realized I had much more to learn about teaching my own baby. I found books such as *Baby Learning Through Baby Play, How to Raise a Brighter Child, The First Three Years of Life,* and many more. I learned that "famil-

I had so much fun, and my baby had so much fun.

iarity," "repetition," and "begin at the beginning" should begin earlier than even the first grade; in fact, children should be exposed to these themes right away—in infancy. Soon I was busily involved creating baby toys that would be fun to use and would promote the learning of basic concepts at the same time. I had so much fun with this project, and my baby had so much fun; but the bonus came when she was about two years old. At that time I realized that she already knew all the letters of the alphabet, numbers from one to ten, about ten colors, basic shapes, and more. She was even recognizing whole words and reading them!

The approach I used was basic enough for any parent to follow, and would benefit any child. In my case, because my daughter was diagnosed at birth to have Down's syndrome, I was especially delighted with the results. Soon friends in my neighborhood began to notice my daughter's advanced academic knowledge. They wondered how this child could have mastered so many skills, of which most children her age were unaware. Friends started coming over to see the toys I had made and to learn how to make and use them with their own children. Eventually a friend of mine remarked, "If I get the people together and if I use my house, would you give us some lessons on how to make educational toys for our kids?" Who could say no to that!

Before long, I began teaching neighborhood workshops to interested groups of parents. Soon after that I developed a handbook to go with the course. That handbook had several lives and eventually became this book. *Baby and Toddler Learning Fun* is accessible to parents, caregivers, and preschool teachers and is an easy-to-use guide into the world of toys and play for children from birth to age three. Parents, caregivers, and teachers can use this resource on their own, in classes, or in neighborhood parenting groups.

The activities and toys in this book have withstood the test of hundreds of parents and their babies and have consistently provided opportunities for meaningful parent-child interactions. These play activities give parents real support in their efforts to provide an enriched environment for their child during a significant early stage of the baby's development, especially in boosting language, motor, and social skills.

This book is divided into three parts. Part 1 presents ideas to keep in mind as you make the toys and use them in play with your child. These ideas will help you make the most of the play experience and will help you invent new ways to make your entire home a fruitful place for early learning. Part 2 gives instructions for making and using fifty simple toys, quickly and easily. Remember that these are *your family's* toys—go ahead and decorate them as you please. Be prepared to discover a creative streak you didn't know you had! Finally, Part 3 provides followup activities and an overview.

Taken as a whole, this book shows parents simple and effective ways to enrich their baby's environment every single day. The activities in this book reflect a way of looking at the world on your baby's behalf during this remarkable time of his growth and development. My guess is that once you try these activities you will be eager to experiment with your creativity in other areas of play and learning with your child. Once you start to work with the toys in this book, all sorts of other engaging activities are likely to occur to you to try in the natural course of your day. You may find yourself spontaneously counting out with your baby how many pieces of mail the mail carrier delivered; naming the animals you see when you take a walk together, from "little bug" to "pretty bird"; and so much more!

The activities in this book reflect a way of looking at the world on your baby's behalf during a remarkable time of his growth and development.

You'll soon realize that almost every interaction you have with your baby is an opportunity to help your baby learn more about his world. The activities in this book will help you learn how to use the concepts of familiarity, repetition, and "begin at the beginning" to reinforce the learning your baby is already doing just by observing and testing his world. Your baby will love communicating with you in such a special way—and you'll love it too.

SRG

Introduction

This book is written for you to use soon after your child is born—immediately after, if you like!—continuing until your child reaches about age three. Because the techniques I describe enhance a child's learning potential, they may be of particular interest to parents of children with delayed development or learning disabilities.

You will find in these pages good ideas for providing a positive, enriched environment for your child right from the start—the kind of environment that enhances a desire for learning and at the same time brings you closer together. You'll find stimulating activities that you and your child will enjoy together and toys that are easy to make, fun to use, and effective in accomplishing specific learning objectives. There are several key developmental areas, which I will discuss shortly. These ideas are truly "child's play," but with an important difference: They provide not only toy-making instructions but also much-needed advice, background, and direction for using them in play with your child. The time you spend playing with your child as a result will be as rewarding as possible—for both of you!

A Book for Parents

This book is for working as well as at-home moms—and dads too! Whether they work outside the home or inside it, parents usually have limited free time and limited budgets. The toys you will learn to make in this book are easy to make in a short amount of time. Perhaps in the past you've shopped at toy

Most of what you will need can be found right in your own home.

stores for your baby, only to be disappointed by his lack of enthusiasm for the item you bought and frustrated to think you had spent so much time choosing a toy that didn't work out. I will show you exactly how to get the most fun and learning from every toy you create. Toys you make yourself are also budget-friendly toys.

Perhaps to your surprise, you will find that you do not need to buy much in the way of materials to make creative toys, and most of what you will need can be found right in your own home.

All of the toys and play ideas in this book are for children during the years from birth to age three, but many will continue to be interesting to your child for several years after that. During the first year, the idea is just to put these toys where your baby can experience them easily. Your natural explanations and interactions in showing the toy are all that is necessary at this time. Your baby will become familiar with the toys by looking at them and manipulating them. During baby's second year, watch her curiosity take over as she explores everything in sight! Your toddler will take more initiative with the toys, playing with them in new ways. During baby's third year, you will notice she uses the toys for more purposeful play.

One of the richest aspects of this book is that all the suggestions for play contribute to helping you develop a meaningful relationship with your child. The parent-child relationship is the first and most important relationship a child will have. Its power is especially great during the first three years, and it will have a lasting effect on all future relationships. By making the toys with which your child plays, you bring an extra dimension of love and intimacy to the play. Your love for your child is ex-

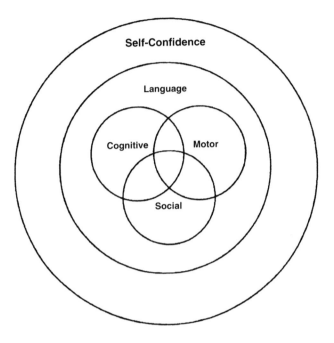

The Picture of Development

pressed anew in the toys you make for him, and that love will extend into your play together.

Learning at Home Is Natural

The toys in this book address six specific areas—self-awareness, colors, letters, numbers, shapes, and reading. These are basic academic concepts that help children sort out the complicated world in which they live. If, as we know, children learn first and best in the home environment, why not arrange that environment so that it reinforces these concepts? Just as children learn to recognize their parents, brothers, sisters, and friends, and just as they learn the names of their own toys and stuffed animals, so they can learn colors, letters, numbers, shapes, and words. Just as they memorize storybooks about Mickey Mouse, Barney, and Cinderella, so they can memorize books about colors, letters, numbers, shapes, and reading. Learning from toys can be quite natural. Here are some tried and tested techniques.

Self-Awareness

Personalized Room Deco (page 93), is a room-decoration scheme you can make for your child. In a personalized room, your child finds his name on display, so he can study the way it is written. His picture is in view in a wall hanging as a reminder of his importance, and the photo is updated frequently to show how quickly he grows (page 94). Over time, you'll notice that the accumulated photographs show an interesting sequence of events. Remove all the pictures from the wall hanging from time to time and show them to your child. By laying them on a table in sequential order, your child has an opportunity to see how he has grown from a small baby to his present size. What a statement of self-awareness!

Colors

This book contains a rich selection of toys about color. Each was developed according to the different ways that infants, one-year-olds, and two-year-olds naturally play. For example, all babies play with containers that they love to empty and fill. Now your child can play with Color Boxes: red, yellow, blue, and green containers filled with red, yellow, blue, and green objects (page 102). These containers can range in size from pint and quart to half-gallon ice-cream containers, with colored lids that you add yourself. For slightly older babies, make a Color Book in each primary color (page 105). The Red Book, for example, features red pages and pictures of red objects (such as red apples), and so on, for each color. Color Cards give toddlers another opportunity to think about color (page 108). Color

Cards show the color word written in the color on one side and written in black on the other. These toys are easy for your child to carry wherever she goes. What's more, anyone else who picks up the materials to play with your child and says the color teaches and reinforces the color concepts with ease. Colors toys and activities are discussed in Chapter 8.

Letters

Letters are just as much fun for your child to learn as colors, and just as easy for him. For each letter of his name, you can make or buy a pillow in the shape of that letter. These stuffed "letter pillows" can be as much fun to hug and to hold as stuffed animals (page 126). You can also collect office file boxes and then place a different stick-on letter to each side of the box (page 118). Use these boxes for storing toys. Parents, you can use the letter on the top of each box to remember which box you brought out most recently; rotate your child's toys to keep interest high. Just through playing with the toys and the repetition of using these Letter Toy Boxes, your child will become familiar with letters. Create Letter Cards that hang on a high chair, hooks, or door handles, and you'll have another creative way to help your child learn his letters (page 114).

Becoming familiar with these cards is just like becoming familiar with anything else. It is no harder for a little child to learn to recognize a "B" than it is for him to learn to recognize a spoon, fork, or cup—it may even be easier! See Chapter 9, "Toys About Letters."

Numbers

Let numbers become a way of life around your house. First, find them easily on food containers and throughout newspapers and magazines, sharing all of them with your baby and calling them by name ("Look, there's a 'nine'!"). Second, count anything and everything—spoons, paper cups, pieces of mail, pens, pencils, and more. Do not forget that ten fingers and toes are always only seconds away!

Shapes

You'll soon notice that basic shapes are *all around you*. Once you start looking at the world in terms of shapes, it will be hard to stop. Almost all of your books and magazines will become rectangles or squares in your mind's eye. Simple things like napkins are squares, and how easily they can be folded into triangles! CDs are circles. Shape hunting with your baby can be a lot of fun.

Reading

Can reading really be taught as part of a baby's routine? You may be surprised to learn the answer is yes. Start reading to your baby even before he can sit up. Storytime before sleep is a good place to begin. As you read, hold your baby close and point to each word in the book with your finger, indicating from the beginning that those printed words on the page are telling you what to say. Start with short, simple books, which can be homemade, with one picture or one picture and one word on a page (page 83). Gradually introduce two words per page, then one sentence, two sentences, and so on. Find or make books with large print so that you can continue to reinforce the idea that the printed words have meaning (page 90).

New research shows that babies can say and also read their first words. Each time your baby says a new word, write it down in large letters on a standard piece of notebook paper or on a five-by-eight-inch index card. Show your baby the word and read it to him. Then bind four or five of these word pages together to make your toddler a book of his own first words. As your child's speaking-and-reading vocabulary develops, make new books up to ten pages long. You might even add a front cover that says "Book" and a plain back cover.

It takes one, two, or three showings of a particular word for your child to retain it as real reading vocabulary. A high-interest word takes fewer repetitions than a word that is not as interesting to him. As time goes by, you can expect your child to remember *all* the words.

A Book for Caregivers

If you are a caregiver, you will find that the toys in this book create equally meaningful play opportunities for the children in your care. You can also teach the parents of the children you care for how to make the toys as part of stimulating parent workshops. Think about partnering with parents by asking them to bring in some of the household items needed to make the toys, and then conduct a make-your-own toy program with them and their children.

Teaching with Toys in a Child-Care Setting

As a caregiver working in a child-care center, you have a wonderful opportunity to teach with toys. Your room may already contain many toys and objects that teach these concepts. Collect and sort them. Keep toys together that relate to the same learning concerns. An unsorted mix of toys can look confusing to young children, but toys grouped by category can become quite meaningful to them. You might decide to group toys according to the concepts of educational development as described below.

Self-Awareness

Set up a place in the room where you place Name Cards (page 81) for each baby or toddler. Keep homemade books created for each child that are called "My Family" and "My Story" (page 86) in the same section. In addition, hang the Personalized Room Decos for each child here as well (page 93). Display mirrors so the children can see their reflection while they play in this part of the room. You might hang large mirrors on the wall and put out unbreakable hand mirrors for play. This area makes a wonderful spot to hang Toy Bags for each infant or toddler (page 100). A Toy Bag keeps a child's personal toys separate from other children's toys. It also teaches these small children a sense of where things belong and the idea of putting items back in their own designated places. See Chapter 7 for pictures and information about these types of toys.

Most of what you will need can be found right in your own home.

Colors

You are certain to create excitement when you designate a special area of the playroom just for colors. Let your creativity run wild! Use plastic crates in different colors to store toys of the same color. Use shelf space to store individual Color Boxes, Color Books, and Color Cards (pages 102, 105, and 108). Hang color pictures and even colored items such as plastic silverware, plates, and paper cups on bulletin boards.

Why not choose certain days for the children to dress in the "Color of the Day"? They can also bring in color items for that particular day. A caregiver can dress in the color too and point out objects throughout the day that reflect the designated color. Color days create quite a lot of conversation for parents, caregivers, and children as they all collaborate to create a uniform color effect.

Letters

Letter toys lend themselves well to special sections of the room. Coat hooks are excellent for hanging Letter Cards (page 114). Letter Toy Boxes (page 118) provide another way of storing toys, this time according to the first letter in the toy's name. They also provide a natural system for rotating toys. ("Today let's play with toys beginning with the letter 'D,' as in 'doll.'") Children can play with Letter Notebooks stored on a low shelf in an attractively designed letter area (page 124). Store all the different alphabet blocks in this part of the room as well, and display letter pillows prominently on a wall. Arrange them in ABC order, as words or as children's names. Vary the combinations as often as you wish. Toddlers have great fun using letter pillows to write out their names. Refer to Chapter 9 for more letter toy ideas.

Numbers

The number toys are books and cards. They are easily stored on a low shelf. The beauty of the Number Books is that they are designed to be used one at a time (page 134). The advantage of the Sort o' Cards is that they can also be used one by one (page 137). These toys are surprisingly simple to make and, along with the many number activities suggested in Chapter 10, are very effective for teaching children to recognize and understand numerals.

Shapes

Making a section for shape toys could be helpful. Parents and their children can make Shape Books for the child-care center (page 150). Invite them to create Shape Boxes too (page 153). Pile up Word Puzzles (page 183) and add the Shape Seats (page

160) for a nice addition to a "Color of the Day" activity. Shape toys are illustrated and discussed in Chapter 11.

Reading

A reading area is a must for any child-care center. This should come complete with a small library and a comfortable place for reading. There is no specific way this should be set up because it depends on the resources and what room is available. Resources could be beanbag chairs, carpet mats, a couch or comfortable chair, or some other cheerful yet relaxing setup. Besides the regular reading books, consider creating an inviting display of homemade books. Individual Word Books can go there (page 169), and so can personal Word Notebooks (page 172). The Categories Book is another worthwhile addition, and the Word Card File Box for play also fits in well here (pages 175 and 198). See Chapter 12 for ideas about many different toys that you can make for reading activities.

Whether at home or in a center, the personalized toys that you make yourself provide infants and toddlers with meaningful educational experiences. Taking a relaxed approach to teaching and using a variety of simple but interesting household items accelerates learning for any child. Taking care and providing a sense of order and control over all the toys sets up an effective learning environment.

Part ONE

Teaching with Toys

1

Toys, Play, and Learning

The Five Senses

All humans connect with our world through our five senses, beginning in infancy and continuing throughout our lives. Your child is using these tools right now to learn everything he can about the world around him. In the beginning, sight, sound, taste, and smell are important. Before long, as your baby begins to grasp and then reach for objects, the sense of touch becomes important. So when you make toys for your baby, gear them to one or more of the five senses. Because taste and smell are well covered at mealtime, concentrate on activities involving sight, sound, and touch. "Does baby have something to see, to hear, or to touch?" is a good question

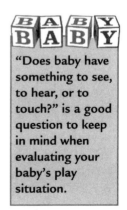

"Does baby have something to see, to hear, or to touch?" is a good question to keep in mind when evaluating your baby's play situation.

to keep in mind when evaluating your baby's play situation. If you see your baby looking at four blank sides of a crib or bassinet, hang a mobile overhead or slip a few brightly colored pictures into the side of the crib. Magazine covers are an excellent source of eye-catching designs and large expressive faces. Even a tiny baby is ready for pictures to enjoy. (When your baby is old enough to chew on the pages, however, discontinue their use.)

Finding and Making Toys

A helpful way to encourage your baby to learn about his environment is to alter that environment in an interesting way every so often. Toys play an important role in this effort, but to do their job, they don't have to be expensive or have a lot of frills, like so many of the toys you buy in stores. You may be surprised by the simple household items that make wonderful baby toys without any modification at all.

The key to choosing and making toys for baby is to be aware that he appreciates variety in his environment. If your baby is in a playpen surrounded by several large plastic toys, you may wish to add a few small, textured items he can play with for a change of pace. You might throw in a net bag from oranges or grapefruits, for example. (Be sure to cut off the large staple at the bottom.) Little fingers will love the texture. Your baby is not likely to try to swallow the netting, but don't leave your baby alone with it. Other light household items that babies like a lot include

- plastic measuring cups (fun for stacking and nesting)
- high-quality fabric ribbon (such as grosgrain), six inches to a foot in length and knotted at both ends so that it will not unravel (fun to pull and wave)

- fluffy yarn pom-poms (They feel so good!)
- small plastic containers (good for stacking and opening)
- paper (Babies love the satisfying crinkle sound it makes when crumpled.)

The list is almost endless. Open your pantry and cupboards, and go from there. Some household items are fine to use just as they are, and others can be adapted slightly to teach specific learning skills. By using readily available household items and a few basic cut-and-paste materials, you can make all sorts of meaningful toys for infants, toddlers, and young children. For more toys, you can easily pick up additional materials from drugstores and office supply and discount stores. For parts that you buy and toys that you make, always check the toy carefully to be sure it is something that is safe for your baby. Let's consider those important safety considerations next.

Safety First!

Before giving your child any toy or beginning any play activity, first put on your "safety glasses" and make sure that whatever you give your baby can't harm him. Here are some important cautions:

- Be sure that the toy has no small pieces that he could pull off and swallow (such as buttons used as eyes on some stuffed animals or dolls), no sharp edges, and no strings long enough for your baby to wrap around his neck.
- Check for unprotected staples, dyes, and toxic glues.
- Don't let baby chew on foil, wrapping paper, or magazine paper. Ask yourself if a toy made with any of these materi-

als could be used in such a way that baby might chew it. If so, don't use it.

- Use clear contact paper or lamination to cover parts to make toys safe, as well as to make them more durable. Photos, which I recommend frequently in this book, can be covered with contact paper (such as Con-Tact brand transparent paper) or laminated so that any chemicals present, such as those found at the bottom of some brands of instant-developing film, cannot be released.
- Use nontoxic markers for all projects.
- Check toys regularly for signs of wear. Each time you give your child a toy to play with, look it over carefully first to see if any part of it is broken or damaged. Has a sharp edge developed? Has the protective laminate covering peeled away? It may be time to replace the toy.

Interactive Learning

This book is designed to be a handbook for parents and caregivers of children from birth to age three. It shows how to provide academic stimulation before the preschool years. Although the playthings suggest a certain focus on academic areas (thinking skills), the interactive ways the toys are used offer plenty of opportunity to enhance baby's development in other areas as well—motor, social, language, and self-confidence.

Learning with toys takes advantage of the way in which your baby naturally plays at different stages and channels it into an enriching experience. The toys and activities in this book are specifically *not* intended to modify play or to require your baby to spend extra time working on "lessons." To the contrary, these toys are just plain fun to play with, with the added benefit of guiding your child to an understanding of a few basic concepts.

Once this distinction is established and understood, the question "Why teach your baby certain academic skills?" becomes "Why not?" The six basic concept categories of self-awareness, colors, letters, numbers, shapes, and reading can be introduced as early as you wish and built upon in lots of interesting ways as your child grows.

Throughout this book, you will learn ways to make toys that aid a baby's early understanding of concepts in these six categories. Babies will use the toys in one way, of course, and toddlers in others. Unlike most store-bought toys, the versatile toys you make yourself will keep your child's interest as he grows! These toys will become very familiar to your child and will be used over and over. As we know, familiarity and repetition are key to effective early learning.

In today's technological society, computers have become a large part of the play-and-learn scene for even the youngest children. All kinds of computer games and activities are available that can keep young children occupied for long periods. Many of these computerized play activities are educational. It's common these days to compare slick new computer activities against the simple games and activities that parents have used to interact with their babies for hundreds of years. Many parents wonder: Should modern computer games replace the slower-paced, homemade activities we grew up with? Would that be better for our children and help prepare them for a rapidly changing future? As it happens, where early childhood development is concerned, the old ways may still be the best ways. Let's see why.

Learning is a complex activity, and in early childhood particularly real learning requires input from five diverse developmental areas, called cognitive, motor, social, language, and self-confidence. Each developmental area is equally important, as the illustration on page xv shows. As we will see, computer play-and-learn games, although fine in some circumstances,

cannot substitute for the diverse experiences a parent can provide. In these areas interacting in even very simple ways is
meaningful to a child. Let's look at each area individually.

The Five Areas of Learning

Cognitive Development—All About Learning.   Learning is based
on what the child experiences *himself*. Researchers in this area
say that people tend to remember 10 percent of what they hear,
50 percent of what they see, and fully *90 percent* of what they
do. Children have an inborn curiosity that stimulates them to
explore their world using their senses—hearing, seeing, tasting,
smelling, and touching. They grasp concepts about *big and
small, heavy and light, over and under,* and others through what
they actually see, hear, touch, taste, and smell.

A child who spends a lot of time in front of a personal computer tends to emphasize his visual sense at the expense of the
other senses. For a very young child, a short walk in the park
with a parent provides him with much more sensory feedback
than an afternoon spent in front of a computer screen. The toys
in this book will also provide numerous opportunities for your
child to look at, touch, smell, and listen to as you play together.

Motor Development—All About Movement.   Motor development
refers to the development of coordinated movement of the body,
particularly the arms and legs ("gross-motor skills") and the
hands and fingers ("fine-motor skills"). All development takes
place in a sequence. When a baby or young child is given large,
open areas to play in, gross-motor development proceeds rapidly
in a predictable, sequential pattern. When a baby is not given
adequate opportunities to crawl, walk, run, and jump, these gross-
motor developmental milestones will be delayed. Fine-motor development follows the same principle. The more opportunities

the child has to use his hands and manipulate objects with his fingers, the faster motor development will take place. Clay, play dough, pegs and pegboards, pencils, blocks, markers, and eventually scissors all play a role in strengthening and developing the small-muscle groups in the hands. Without these kinds of important manipulative experiences, a child's fine-motor development will be delayed. A child who uses a personal computer for long periods may not take advantage of a very special time in his life to explore the world around him through physical play. He is a child who sits a lot. He may use certain fine-motor skills while typing on the keyboard or using a joystick, but these movements are fairly limited and repetitive. He may be deprived of time he might have spent with toys that delight his senses—from fluffy stuffed animals to rough wooden blocks and the stiff pages of his very own storybook.

Social Development—All About Relationships.   The family is the training ground for all future relationships and makes its most significant contribution during the child's first five years of life. As we might expect, the first and most important relationship a baby establishes is the parent-child relationship. Next most important to baby's social development is her relationship with grandparents, followed by her relationship with brothers and sisters. After the immediate family, aunts, uncles, and cousins also provide important early relationships, as well as relationships established with close friends of the family. You might imagine these relationships as similar to the ever-widening circles that radiate out from a pebble thrown into a pond. The circles closest to the center are the most important, but all the circles together complete the picture. Even for infants, play at the computer is largely a solitary rather than social experience. A computer responds as it is programmed to do, no more, no less. It obviously cannot establish a rewarding relationship with a child.

Language—All About Communication.   The purpose of language is to deliver a message. The purpose of sending a message is to get a reaction. The purpose of the reaction is to communicate another message. The person sending the message uses *expressive language;* the person receiving the message responds using *receptive language.* As they grow, children need lots of extended opportunities to talk (use expressive language), listen (use receptive language), write (use expressive language), and read (use receptive language). Schools today place a great deal of attention on reading; yet talking, listening, and writing skills must also play major roles in the school curriculum for young children. Giving your child plenty of opportunities to spend time with other children in a guided and supportive atmosphere is an excellent way to accomplish these goals. Television, videos, and movies, which display language freely, do not allow adequately for responses and interaction. Computers are also less educational as a communications tool than they may appear at first. Although they allow for controlled responses and interaction, they limit young users to limited visual communication only. Moreover, interaction with a machine lacks the personal and emotional experience that is so vital to normal human development, especially in early childhood: Machines cannot provide eye contact, a warm touch on the arm, or a smile! Human expression and response are the vital components that make speaking, listening, writing, and reading basic *interactive* processes. Playing with your child is the most natural way in the world to enhance her communication skills.

Self-Confidence—All About Feeling Worthy.   Parents hold the key to a child's feeling of self-worth, and it is almost fully developed in the first few years of life. Unlike a computer, a parent can help establish healthy self-confidence in a child by keeping in mind the following:

- Show respect and appreciation. We show respect by using the word "please." Instead of issuing directives such as "Put that away," say, "Please put that on the shelf." Be sure to acknowledge your child's efforts to comply with "Thank you."
- Comment on uniqueness. Each person who is born is unique. As a parent, you have the gift of witnessing your child's individuality as it unfolds. Take the time to notice your child's special qualities each and every day. Feel free to point them out to your child.
- Gently correct mistaken behavior. Change "misbehavior" to "mistaken behavior" in your vocabulary. Treat your child's errors of social behavior as simple mistakes, not willful defiance. Mistakes are simply opportunities in disguise: Calmly review what happened and why. If your child is very young, you may choose to change the environment somewhat to prevent that problem from repeating itself. If your child is old enough to understand, teach him what to do so the mistake won't happen again.

It *is* possible for a computer to play a limited yet helpful role in each of the developmental areas we have discussed. I recommend that you approach "computer time" with your child with a specific objective in mind. What do you want to accomplish in this time with your child? For example, if you are thinking about teaching colors, the best way to do that is with hands-on experiences such as those in this book involving color boxes, color books, and color cards, not on the computer. To teach reading, on the other hand, play at the computer might be terrific, because a lot of computer software is available to reinforce reading skills. In every case, be critical about what you can and cannot realisti-

Introduce the computer as a supplement to your interactive play with your baby, not as a substitute for it.

cally expect computer play to do for your child's development. Introduce the computer as a supplement to your interactive play with your baby, not as a substitute for it. By choosing carefully when and how to use the computer with your child, you cannot go wrong.

There is no substitute for parent-child involvement or for activities and toys a child can dive into with all of his senses.

Computer play can enhance many educational experiences, but often it will not be as effective as other, more interactive types of activities, because the child's interaction with another person (you!) reinforces the learning that is taking place. There is no substitute for parent-child involvement or for activities and toys a child can dive into with all of his senses. Such enriching activities are at the heart of this book.

Learning

The years from birth to age five are often called the developmental years. Let me be clear: Development is not something anyone can teach a child. However, almost everyone can *facilitate* a child's development; that is, maximize his potential to be all he can be. Development takes place in five areas—cognitive, motor, social, language, and self-confidence (see the illustration on page xv).

All children go through the same developmental stages in more or less the same order. The only difference is that a disadvantaged environment can slow a child's development and an enriched environment can speed it up. That said, every person is different. Each person has a unique genetic makeup and unique health profile that interact with an equally unique set of personal experiences. It is one of life's pleasures in the first five years, especially the first three, to watch your child unfold from a tiny baby to an individual who walks, talks, thinks, and participates in life in a functional way. It is also part of that pleasure to facilitate the process as much as possible.

Learning is intrinsic to the development process. It goes on for your child during every minute of the waking hours. The brain "records over 85 million bits of information every day" (Rick, p. 26). New connections are made as baby sees, hears, touches, tastes, and smells the world around him, and he begins to make relationships out of this information that parents can help facilitate. Because learning takes place, teaching is not the issue. Because you cannot prevent it, it seems only reasonable to do your part in nourishing it. You can provide a positive environment filled with worthwhile experiences to nourish your child's desire to learn.

You do not teach development; you facilitate it.

Unstructured, Individualized Learning

Most of the activities you'll find in this book do not come with a "use by" date. There is no particular age at which to begin using the activities and no particular age at which the toy becomes obsolete for a child from birth to three, either. Use the suggested toys and activities at any time during the foundation years in whatever way your young child guides you. You know best what toys might appeal to your child, and when. As you read about the activities in this book, you may find yourself saying, "That would be perfect for my child right now," or "I think I'll try that in a month or two." There are no hard-and-fast, month-by-month rules for trying these activities. You may even think of a way to modify some of the activities presented here so they will appeal to your child even more. Personalities vary, and so does the learning process for each baby.

By playing with the educational toys described in this book, young children can learn self-awareness, colors, letters, numbers, shapes, some reading, and more, all by the time they are three years old. Many children begin preschool at three and face the challenge of mastering these concepts for the first time. Many five-year-olds throughout the country enter kindergarten without these basic learning concepts and are not what we call "ready for school" as a result. This is a shame, because all the learning that is possible from birth to age three does not require long hours of hard work, which is difficult for both adults and children and certainly is not recommended. On the contrary, such early learning is the direct result of playing with your child with interesting, exciting, and creative toys that stimulate curiosity and experimentation.

Relaxed Time

An inborn desire to learn, call it curiosity, motivates your child to play and experience his world and to find out all he can about it. Unplanned time—the natural condition for early learning—is essential for your child. Such time is rich with spontaneous play. If you are simply available to your baby, offering your time and attention, your child will know exactly what to do to keep himself busy! How nice it is to know that you can let it all happen. Just as there are no official rulebooks for being a parent because nature imbues you with the necessary knowledge to care for your young, so there are no official rulebooks for children. Remember when you were a child? Just as you knew, so does your child.

Family

Your child benefits when you spend time with him and introduce him to a wide variety of experiences and activities. All

FIGURE 1.1   Just Being Together

positive experiences play a role in your child's learning and development. However, one-on-one interactions aren't the only kind baby needs. The surrounding family also plays a major role in a child's development. Experts recommend that the family spend as much time together as possible. One way to do this is to make sure everyone shares a meal together at least once a day.

Incidentally, the time spent together as a family does not need to be structured in a particular way all the time. It's just as beneficial for family members to spend time together while pursuing individual activities. For example, the family might be gathered in the family room, with Dad playing a game of solitaire at the table while Mom reads a book to baby on the sofa, and brother and sister play a game on the floor.

Why is it so important to spend time together as a family? Family members literally take care of each other. Life is challenging, and there is always much work to be done to provide adequate

FIGURE 1.2   Father-Child Fun

food, clothing, shelter, and refuge for a family. That group needs to know very well who they are and what they mean to each other. Family relationships, which are by no means easy, are the training ground for all future relationships. It is important for young children during the years from birth to age five, especially birth to three, to have sufficient time interacting with people and developing these essential interpersonal skills.

As you grow as a family and continue to enjoy experiences with each other, remember that you are all unique and different. You all have personal likes and dislikes. You all have skills you are good at and skills that could use a little improvement. That is the beauty of who you all are today and the people you are all evolving into for tomorrow.

There are two inner layers of relationships that help to protect our children. The first is the immediate family—parents, grandparents, and brothers and sisters. Then comes the extended family with aunts, uncles, and cousins. With meaningful, supportive experiences with family members, your child will have the necessary guidance to handle himself in school, community, and social relationships. The family is a working system of people who work together. If one member has a problem, the whole unit has the problem, and the whole unit needs to work together to help that member.

Moreover, these protective experiences will last your child for a lifetime. When he goes through the middle school and high school years, times when he will not be spending a lot of hours in the day with the family physically, he will have the impact of his early family experiences. These experiences will stay with him in a symbolic way for life and continue to provide him with guidance and support.

Home

The Power of the Parent

"Home is where the heart is." The atmosphere you create in your home will stay with your children for their lifetimes. Parenting is the way you express it. You have great power. You are the most important model of behavior that your children will ever know. Even more significant, what you think of your children eventually tells them what they will think of *themselves*. You can send this message subtly or boldly to your child, but you do give it and your child does receive it. Be sure it is a positive message!

Knowing how important your home life is, you might even want to create a mission statement for your family and display it proudly. Many businesses create mission statements as a way of telling others and themselves who they are, their vision for the company, and how they will accomplish goals that reinforce that vision. Mission statements are usually kept on display so that anyone in the business or visiting the company can read them.

A family's mission statement can be just as powerful. It could include thoughts about being a good, positive family in which each member leads a healthful life. It could say that courteous behavior and high integrity are family priorities. It can say whatever you want it to say about the way you want your family to be. Use it as a form of guidance for each family member for each and every day.

It takes time to create a mission statement. You may go through several drafts before you settle on the description that is just right for your family. Once you have finished it, be sure to place it somewhere in the home where everyone can see it easily. You might consider posting it where you and other family members can add other motivational messages to it. The idea behind the mission statement is to provide a vision of the future that everyone in the family can support and work toward. It is hard to "get there" if you do not know "exactly where you are going." A good mission statement provides that road map.

The Power of the First Three Years

In 1975, Harvard University professor Burton White reported in his landmark book, *The First Three Years of Life*, that if a child is well developed in all areas—cognitive, motor, social, language, and self-confidence—by the time he is three, he is much more likely than other children his age to be successful in school by age six. White backed up this statement with his research findings. He found that children need high-quality experiences to become well developed. High-quality experiences are filled with nurturing love, guidance, support, protection, and educational stimulation. The logical follow-up to this important finding is to provide every parent with the information they need to provide such experiences to their baby. Since 1975, the year the findings were reported, this information has been made available to parents in a piecemeal fashion at best. Unfortunately, no coordinated national program yet reaches out to every parent and child to provide them with the information they need and the resources to help them make use of it.

In 1994, the Carnegie Commission completed a multimillion-dollar study designed to learn some of the reasons we suffer so much crime and violence in our country. According to the commission's report, what happens to children in the first three years can be the key to unlocking a propensity for crime and violence later in life. One can only conclude that some children who are deprived of nurturing love, guidance, support, protection, and educational stimulation in the first three years are those who turn to crime and violence later. Clearly, there is some urgency to providing the finest experiences during the years from birth to three for every baby born in our country.

The information in this book brings the whole issue of providing high-quality experiences for babies to a practical level any parent or caregiver can use. It provides parents with guidelines and then provides them with suggestions for how to carry them out. The idea is to use simple materials like scissors, paper, index cards, crayons, markers, and plastic containers and turn them into toys that are fun to use. This book is interactive in the very best way: Parents like to use the toys because of the creativity they have put into them, and their children like the toys because their parents use them to spend more time playing with them. I hope you will benefit from this book and enjoy sharing it with others who can benefit from it as well.

Guidance from Research

Thanks to long-term studies started more than fifty years ago at Harvard University by Burton White, director of Harvard's well-known Pre-School Project, we know a lot today about the best ways to handle infants and toddlers. White's thirty years of research, completed in 1975, gave us the information we needed to give babies the best start possible in life.

White is credited with finding out that babies smile at human faces or things that look like them. During the first six weeks of life, maybe as early as the first week, a baby looks toward the eyes of the person holding him and even toward the eyes in a picture of a human face. From birth, your baby wants to look at your face as much as possible. From this single finding, we know how important it is for parents to be available to their babies as much as possible during the first years of life. Since his book was published in 1975, other researchers have built on White's important work and have brought us additional insights about how babies learn about their world.

You will find many references to research in this book. However, please remember that parents have reared children successfully since the beginning of mankind, even without

When a baby is born, parents are born too.

books to follow! Just as all other animals know instinctively how to take care of their young, so do human parents. When a baby is born, parents are born too. At that moment they are imbued with great wisdom and an almost supernatural power to do anything and everything necessary to take care of their child. Remaining close to nature is key. Listening to your inner voice and the added wisdom of loved ones has always been helpful. Now with today's fast-paced lifestyle, often away from the support of grandparents, you have a quick and easy reference and many ways to make personalized and individualized play experiences for your child.

Guidance from Mother Nature

Even with our apparent distance from nature, her influence has by no means disappeared. Many parents have incredible insight. They read parenting books and say to themselves, "I did that." "I knew that." "I love that." You may be such a parent yourself.

Music

If your baby is in an infant seat looking out the window, why not enrich that experience and put on soft music in the background? Think about the music you especially want your child to know and enjoy, and keep examples of it in your home (and perhaps in your car as well). Classical music is wonderful for starting. Since it is our most refined music, introduce that first and let it become the standard. Most people like the music of composers such as Chopin, Beethoven, and Mozart, so you might begin with them. Brahms is especially soothing for ending the day.

When you introduce classical music to your baby, choose one composer or even just one recording to play over the course of several days or weeks. When you think your child recognizes some of the complex melodies of that piece, introduce another composer or recording. Take advantage of making classical music the background of your day by keeping a radio tuned softly to a classical music station. Listening to music doesn't always have to be a "background" activity, however, no matter what kind you like. Make it a purposeful activity of its own also. Enhance music time with nursery rhymes and other children's music of your choice.

2

Why Make Your Own Toys?

If all the toys you needed for your child were in stores at prices you could afford, it *would* be easier to go out and buy them instead of making them yourself. But oddly enough, with all the toys you can buy in stores, in most cases the best toys aren't available! Throughout this book, you will learn the best kinds of toys that your child will love and learn from, and you will find out that most of those toys are not for sale, even at a high price.

The developmental toys appearing in six categories in this book—self-awareness, colors, letters, numbers, shapes, and reading—give you an idea of the qualities to look for when you buy toys as well as when you make them. Similar to food groups, these "toy groups" can help you provide a well-rounded play experience for your child.

Buying Toys

It is a good idea to make a toy list, much as you would a grocery list, before going to the toy store. Toy packaging, which is so attractive, can catch your eye and lure you into making unnecessary purchases. By making a list beforehand, you will be able to leave extra toys behind and arrive home with exactly what you *do* need.

Making Toys

You'll find a lot of satisfaction in making something for your child. One mother remarked after making a few of the toys in this book, "Until now, the only creative thing I had ever done was having my two children." (She went on to make many more toys and also to have another child.) Busily engrossed in making one of the alphabet toys, another mother said, "My two older daughters kept asking me last night if they could help me, and I kept telling them I wanted to do it myself. Don't ask me why." "Why," I answered, "because you want to create."

We have known for a long time that making a toy for your baby does *not* mean trying to make it look like a store-bought toy. At a toy exhibition, the 1979 Arango International Design Competition in Miami, Florida, most entries sported sophisticated designs—but despite that, the winner was a set of forty wooden tongue depressors, each painted on one end with a different brightly colored picture. There was a snowman, a sun, an ice-cream cone, and similar familiar objects common to the life of a child. To play, the child would pick his own sticks, arrange them in his own order, and tell a story with them. For example, "I bought an ice-cream cone for my friend the snowman, but the sun came out and melted him, so I ate it."

FIGURE 2.2 What Do You See!

a wealth of treasures. Some items can be used as they are and others can be embellished to make wonderful playthings. Your collection may include simple containers in different sizes— quarter-pound, half-pound, and one-pound; pint, quart, and half-gallon sizes. With lids on, these containers are fun to stack. Without lids, they are fun to nest. Filled with bottle caps or other simple objects, such as paper clips or plastic spoons, they are fun to shake. On other occasions you may find bottles with various interesting shapes. Consider the variety of shapes in milk, water, juice, and even mouthwash containers. These too can be filled and become shakers.

This is the toy box for the twenty-first century!

An old-time favorite is a half-gallon plastic milk container filled with ten clothespins for your baby to empty and fill. Toddlers have been playing with toys like these for generations. Believe it or not, they used to be made of glass and filled with

FIGURE 2.3   The Recycle Bin

wooden clothespins. You can feel lucky to have the safety of our modern plastic version.

Some containers can be converted into manipulative toys, which help baby develop his fine-motor (hand) skills. Remember the old wooden "mailbox" toys that came complete with blocks in different shapes? You would drop the blocks through their matching cutouts at the top of the "mailbox" and be rewarded by a lovely "thud" as the block fell through the hole and into the mailbox. You can make the same kind of toy at home by using old plastic containers with lids. By cutting a shape in the lid to match an object on hand—such as a circle cut out to match the size of a bottle cap, or a square the size of a small wooden block, or a triangle from a shape-sorter toy or from a wooden building-block set—you have created a wonderful toy for dropping things into! In the beginning, your baby will enjoy holding the objects in any way he can; later he will enjoy putting the cap in the circle very precisely. Soon, two cutouts on one lid can be used to practice putting the correct shape in

FIGURE 2.4   A Toy Known for Generations

FIGURE 2.5   Shapes

FIGURE 2.6   Boxes

the right place. Still later, all three shapes can be used at once on one big lid.

Boxes

Think of how many boxes of one size or another that you throw out each day! Some make great toys just as they are. Shoe boxes are sturdy and come in all sorts of colors and designs. They all have lids for babies to put on and take off.

Books

Other boxes show big, colorful pictures of their contents, such as food or toys. You can cut out those pictures and paste them

FIGURE 2.7   Books

on construction-paper pages and form them into three-ring folder books. You might want to make a whole book about food or one about your baby's own toys. If you end up with a lot of pictures and a lot of pages, you might want to make a thicker book in a three-ring binder.

You can put words in these books as well. For a start, you might make one-word or two-word labels, or simple three-, four-, or five-word sentences. When writing a sentence, be sure to start the sentence with a capital letter and end it with a period. When you read the books to your child, point to each word as you say it. Examples might be "See the shoes," "Cereal," "Pretty candlesticks."

What about a book about your child's friends? Collect pictures of children in the neighborhood or your child's child-care program, put them on colored paper, mount the pages in a folder, and you have a book about friends. You can cover these pages with clear contact paper, laminate them, or put the whole book into a photo album.

As you read any of these books to your baby, point to the picture and then to the label.

FIGURE 2.8   My Friends

FIGURE 2.9   Photo Books

Can you think of another kind of book you would like to make? Maybe you have pictures from a trip that you would like to share over and over with your child. Put only one picture on each page and one label. As you read any of these books to your baby, point to the picture and then to the label. In this way, your child will learn that they both represent the same thing. If you decide to make your books in small photo albums, you can put your pictures on the right-hand sides and the words that go with the pictures on index cards on the left-hand sides of the open pages. If you are using large photo albums, you can place your pictures in the center of the pages and put descriptive words under the pictures.

A Variety of Toys

Once you start making a few toys, you will find yourself making more and more, and seeing the possibility of making toys out of all kinds of common household objects. You may find yourself looking creatively at the ten paper cups in your cupboard, for example. Give them to your toddler and describe them as ten paper cups. What better way to learn about "ten" than to see and feel it as a toy? When one cup is broken or torn, throw it away and show your child that now there are  "nine." Stack them, count them, divide them—do whatever comes to mind. Keep replacements on hand and you have a ready-made, fabulous toy for toddlers.

Sure, you could buy a lot of commercial toys and books to keep your baby busy, but after making your own toys for baby, you will probably notice very quickly that not too many of them are "just right." You'll discover that the toys you make from what you find around the house, on the other hand, are

FIGURE 2.10   Paper Cups

personal and versatile. In addition, you will derive much satisfaction from being creative as well as resourceful; besides, the price is right!

The toys you make from what you find around the house, on the other hand, are personal and versatile.

In the next chapter, I'll show you ways to network with other parents to keep the creativity flowing. Two heads are better than one when it comes to thinking of new activities and making innovative toys.

3

Toy-Making Workshops

Networking

People have known for generations that "two heads are better than one" and have used "brainstorming" to come up with ideas, solve problems, and create. Today people get together in "Mastermind" groups all over the country. These are groups made up of people with similar interests who want to interact with each other about developing those interests.

A Toy-Making Group

You can benefit from this model and carry it one step farther into a toy-making group. In this kind of group you create the opportunity to help each other design toys for your children and at the same time share child-care ideas. You also gain the opportunity to share supplies related to toy making. You can form this kind of group more or less the same way you would form any other group: For example, you could call people who you think might be interested—parents from your neighborhood or from your baby's child-care center. In addition, contact mothers whom you may know from organizations or associations to which you belong. At-home moms may like this group for the opportunity of having a morning out, along with the chance to make something for their child. Working moms may like it for the opportunity to be in a mothers' group and mix with people who are focused on their children and enriching their children's lives. Such a group will be filled with supportive conversation, the opportunity to make new friends, and even the chance to enjoy a snack or potluck dinner, depending on the arrangements. It will have all the benefits of a networking group with the added attraction of being a creative outlet.

A Place to Meet

Meet in a place appropriate for your group. If yours is a small group, you might meet in each other's homes. Since you plan to be busy making toys, a simple potluck buffet might be a useful idea. If you are in a larger group, you may want to reserve a room in a nearby hotel or restaurant. Often you can make an arrangement to have a meal served to your group for a moderate price.

If you have small babies, you will probably be glad to have your babies with you. Before they can crawl or walk around, they benefit from being in your company and from being with other babies. Once they can move around, they will probably get into your supplies and make your toy-making activity quite a challenge. Time to get a baby-sitter.

The Agenda

Pick any of the six concept categories for a meeting topic—self-awareness, colors, letters, numbers, shapes, or reading—and let each parent know in advance what to bring along. (Part 2 features the toys in chapters for each category, with descriptions, instructions, and a materials list.) You may want to spend several work sessions on one category or skip to another right away.

Waste Not, Want Not

You can find lots of items around the home to save and share for toy-making sessions. These ideas can help you get started:

- Buttons (not too small)
- Ribbon
- Wrapping paper
- Wallpaper samples
- Plastic cake decorations (not sharp!)
- Greeting cards

Always consider your baby's age when you make toys. Some materials are not appropriate for very young babies because they present choking hazards. Don't give a child under three years of age any object to play with that is less than two and a half inches in diameter, which is about the size of the opening of a toilet-tissue tube. Remember that smaller items, such as buttons, attached to a larger toy can come off and still present a choking hazard when a curious child picks them up. Be careful at all times (see page 5).

In addition, you might want to ask group members to start collecting throwaways that could be brought to meetings and used for toys. (See box, this page.) As always, remember to keep a child's age in mind as you collect materials for toy making. Very

FIGURE 3.1   Color Book

small objects are not appropriate for babies (see Safety First! page 5).

Workshop Worksheet

I designed Workshop Worksheet to help parents keep track of the different toys they have made in each of the categories. It's a good idea for everyone in your group to keep such a record, which can also accommodate notes about each project. You can make copies of the chart appearing in the appendix (page 209), or use it as a template for your own version.

Some parents will want to do all of their toy making in these workshops. They will find that babies crying, telephones ringing, paperwork, e-mail, faxes, cooking, family time—and other assorted household responsibilities—make it too difficult to concentrate on designing and making any toys. No matter where and when you decide to do your toy-making work, the Workshop Worksheet will help you work efficiently at your own rate.

Sharing Ideas and Information

Because life has gotten to be quite complicated, and not only when children enter the picture, it is helpful to have a group of parents to turn to for direction and support. Talking to other parents on a regular basis provides an unmatched opportunity to find answers to many of your own parenting questions. So many practical child-development hints and ideas that you would otherwise be totally unaware of can come up in these groups!

One mother I know learned about a publication called *Growing Child* from her group. (You can order this by calling 1-800-927-7289.) The information was especially helpful to her as a first-time mother. It is a newsletter that you can order to match the age in months of your baby. It gives play ideas and other childcare information for the exact age of your child. In addition, the same company publishes *Growing Parent*, another monthly newsletter. This one supports parents on needs, wants, and interests of their own. It gives timely advice and reassurance and includes a monthly calendar of parent-child activities that are creative and educational. The last part of this resource is a third newsletter called *Growing Child Playthings*. This one comes out quarterly and includes recommendations for age-appropriate playthings. The guidance here is toward keepsakes, time-honored traditional toys to play with, learn from, and keep for generations.

It used to be easy to get information about child rearing. It was one benefit of being part of an extended family. Grandparents taught their children who were new parents exactly what they needed to know. Today, however, few grandparents live close enough to their children to advise them. Many others who do live close by are not available to give this kind of guidance because they are too busy with their own lives.

Life is complicated today. In addition to bringing up children, parents are busy doing many different jobs and carrying out many different responsibilities. There are new advances as well. This means that there are new and different considerations and a need to keep up with the times. Child rearing in today's world is not an easy or simple process. Fortunately, toy-making groups are extremely helpful for passing along the kind of important information that new parents frequently need. I have learned that all sorts of useful information is shared at toy-making workshops besides how to make toys, including information about vitamins, teething, sleeping through the night, eating habits, potty training, home remedies, exercise, and much more.

Supplies

When it comes to supplies, working within a group is helpful too. One person may have an abundance of felt and ribbon, another may love glossy magazines and have plenty of colorful pictures to share. Sewing scraps vary from house to house, and they are all great for baby toys. If you must buy something, you can purchase as a group; bulk purchases are usually more economical. (See the Parenting Information section for national stores that generally offer bargains.)

The eyes of a group can often see more clearly than one person alone. At one meeting I know of, a mother brought in a

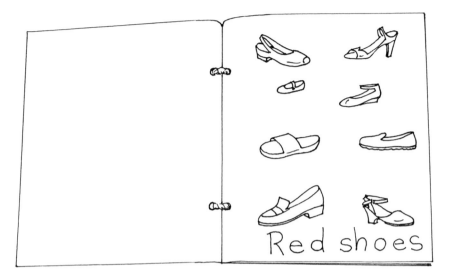

Red shoes

FIGURE 3.2   Color Book

folder for making a Color Book. It was fine except for an envelope section at the bottom, which was not typical of the other
folders that were brought for this activity. Everyone realized at
once that the envelope would be perfect for holding flat items
of the color, which the child could pull out, feel, and put away
again. The items might even be attached to the folder by a
piece of string so that they would not be lost. (Color Books are
described in more detail on page 106.)

Some people may only be interested in making toys from one
category, and others may decide to make only one or two from
each. That's okay! Every parent, child, and situation is different.

A group situation offers good opportunities to learn from others and share information. One mother I know of heard how
well young children in her group were learning their colors,
thanks to Color Boxes, Color Books, and Color Cards. This
news was of particular interest to her because her six-year-old
son, who was attending a special school, was having trouble

learning his colors. The teacher told the boy's mother that there were more important subjects for her son to concentrate on and that "colors would have to wait." Determined that her son should *not* wait, this mother made the entire set of color-section materials for him. She was delighted by how well he learned the colors as a result of their regular playtime together with these toys. (Color toys are discussed in Chapter 8.)

Teaching Appropriately

The secret to using the toys in this book for maximum benefit is simple: *Use them as toys!* It is the nature of these toys to reveal concepts to children during play. Just playing with them in the right way teaches the concepts; using them in the wrong way—for example, as lesson drills—*doesn't* work. The toys you will make are not for giving lessons; the learning comes from your child's exposure to the toys and interaction with them. After making the toys, you use them to engage your child in play.

What is play? Where these toys are concerned, play is as simple and natural as commenting on and describing the toys for your baby, and interacting with your baby to accurately reflect his own experience with the toy. Avoid making playtime feel pressured; it's wise to skip situations in play that require a specific response from your baby or toddler. For example, avoid direct questions such as "What color is this ball?" Just have fun together matching colors that are the same, finding examples of a certain color in objects in the room, and so on.

For example, imagine your baby has been playing for a while with one of the Color Boxes (described on page 102), in which all the objects inside are orange. Imagine you have been naming each object for your baby as she plays: "The orange block, the orange ribbon, the orange ball." After a time, you may start

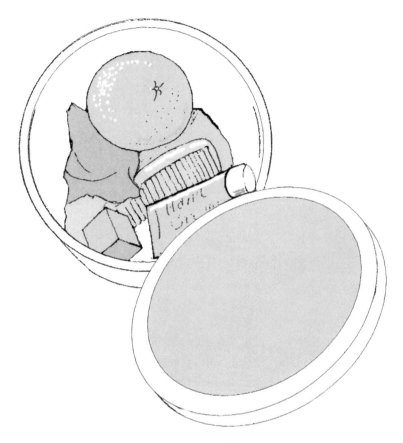

FIGURE 3.3   Color Box

saying something such as "Now you have the orange ribbon. Now you have the orange ball." In time, this naming play can lead into a sentence your toddler can complete for himself, such as "Now you have the . . . block." If your child does not say "orange" the first time you try it, that's okay; don't force him to guess. Maybe he will fill in the blank the next time you say a sentence that is similar. By this approach, you show your child that you are not looking for a "right" answer that bestows approval; rather, you are inviting your child to share the fun of participation in the game.

FIGURE 3.4   Educational Rattle

The First Three Years

Just as you cannot build a house without a foundation, so your child cannot experience optimal growth and development without having the finest experiences in the first three years. Your baby is learning about the world from the moment of birth, and the idea is to have that learning be as positive and as enriched as possible for as long as possible. There is really not a moment to waste. I had my first lesson about this in 1976.

I was shopping in a Finnish furniture store one day, and the salesman showed me a section labeled "Educational Toys for Babies." "What is an educational toy for a baby?" I asked. He took a wooden rattle off the shelf and showed it to me. He then explained that with every other rattle you could buy (at the time), the baby could not see what was making the noise and that with this one, he could. How clear it became to me at that instant that *every* experience is a learning experience meant to be enriched!

The message for toy design and playtime is clear: Your baby does not want you to give him toys that are too simple. Your

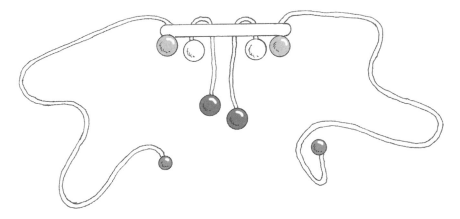

FIGURE 3.5   Cause and Effect

baby is busy every day trying to learn about the world. The more you show it and the less you hide it, the more you are helping the process.

In the same store was another well-designed toy, a rope for hanging across a crib. It was made with four balls that were to dangle into the crib, two red and two green. The design of the crib gym was to stimulate the baby to reach for and pull the balls. It worked like a pulley. If you pulled down on a red one, a green one moved up, and if you pulled down on a green one, a red ball would go up. Concurrently, if you pulled down on one only a little, the corresponding ball would go up only a little. Cause and effect was the lesson, and this toy delivered it well.

A third toy in the store was another version of a crib gym. It was designed to help a baby focus. A small wooden figure sat in the center of a thick rope that stretched across the crib. The figure was made up of small red balls with a simple face drawn on the ball at the top. The face on this toy is the key. As we have seen, babies prefer to look at human faces more than anything else in the world. Without the opportunity to look at a human face, a baby will look at the next best thing, a picture of

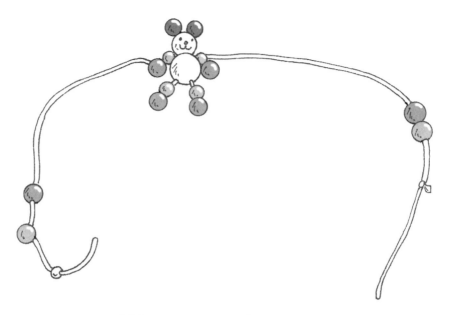

FIGURE 3.6   Toy for Focusing

one. This toy has other attributes that are also of special interest to babies. One is the color red and the other is its round shape.

Providing input and laying an educational groundwork for a child is a continuous, gradual process. Long before your child can talk and express any of her knowledge, she has already learned a lot.

When my daughter was less than six months old, I made a special card for her that was half sandpaper and half smooth paper. I chose black for both papers so that the only thing that was different on each side of the card was the texture. I used to take each one of her little hands and rub them over the card. First I would go over the rough part and say, "rough." Then I would go over the smooth part and say, "smooth." I repeated the procedure with each foot. At some point before she was a year old, the toy was lost, and we stopped that activity. When she was about two years old, she was playing in her room one

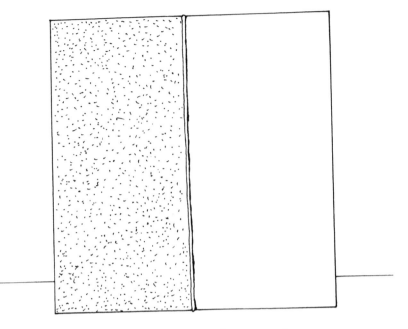

FIGURE 3.7   Rough, Smooth

day and found that toy in her closet. She ran out to me, toy in hand, calling, "Mommy, mommy, rough!" (as she pointed to rough) and "smooth!" (as she pointed to smooth).

Every minute, every hour, every day is important in the life of a child. As parents and caregivers, we have a big responsibility to provide an interesting and meaningful environment for our children. *All* of their experiences are important and have an effect on their development. In the words of Maria Montessori, founder of the successful child-oriented educational system that bears her name, "There is no eraser."

4

Collecting Developmental Ideas

Caring for Children

Caring for children is instinctual. No one has to teach you how to care for your own child. In that realm, *you* are the expert—a true specialist! Basics of childcare—feeding, clothing, and nurturing—have been passed from generation to generation within families.

The great challenge is to do what you know you need to do within the constraints that modern society places on us. Knowing that children need fruit, vegetables, and whole grains for nutrition, for example, and dealing with grocery shelves filled with processed foods is a problem. Knowing that children need daily exercise filled with stretches, muscle building, and cardiovascular activity and dealing with a sedentary school schedule, TV, and computers is a problem. Knowing that children need a regular sleep routine enhanced by going to sleep when it gets dark and waking up at daybreak and having to deal with busy schedules that keep children up very late are problems too. There are others you could name, I'm sure! Aspects of modern life have made many aspects of normal, natural parenting obscure.

In addition, even if you could do all that you know how to do, you would still need guidance on how to do it. Even under the best of circumstances, parenting is tricky, because no two children are alike, and no two parents are alike, either. Parents are learning all the time! And they can learn a lot from other parents.

Each and every parent faces the challenge of finding the appropriate way to handle each one of her children. That requires strategies and techniques as unique as the children they are intended to help. It takes years to learn these skills. Daily life gives you a designated amount of time, money, and energy; the challenge is to use all of those resources in the most effective way.

Record Sheets

As you can see, *getting* lots of good information today is not a problem. The problem is *remembering* it and having it at your fingertips when you need it! With that in mind, I have designed

Following this procedure will help you turn good ideas and good intentions into practice.

worksheets to give you a centralized place to record all of the activities and ideas you would like to try out with your child. You can make copies of the Record Sheet template on page 210 in Appendix B. Make four copies at a time so that you are prepared for an entire month. This worksheet gives you a place to write down, by categories, suggestions you come across that you think will be appropriate for your child. You'll have space on each worksheet to write down several ideas under each category, so you'll be more likely to remember to do them. Record the day or time of day when you followed through with an activity by using the space provided under "days of the week."

For example, maybe you just got back from the doctor's office where you read a fantastic article on child care. You were interested in trying a language-stimulation exercise it mentioned. The exercise suggested naming the parts of the body as you wash each one when you give your child a bath. This practical idea appealed to you because you give your child a bath every day, and it would take no extra time or effort to incorporate the game into that ritual. Writing this suggestion under Language would help you keep track of how often you followed through with your plans.

At the end of the day or during the day, whichever you find more convenient, check off what you have done in each category and write down any new ideas you'd like to try. Following this procedure will help you turn good ideas and good intentions into practice.

The five categories on Record Sheet 1 show five general areas in which your child is growing (see the chart on page 215). Record Sheet 1 is your place for jotting down activities that relate to the five areas of development. Although almost any activity plays a role in all of the five areas, a specific activity usually will focus on one particular area. Record Sheet 1 can help you visualize your goals and help you plan enrichment activities affecting these important areas of your child's development.

The five categories on Record Sheet 2 are focused on schedules and daily activities. Here you can collect suggestions for making a personalized program for your own child. These are ideas that will help your child become all that he can be.

An excellent source of ideas for both sheets is the newsletter program called *Growing Child*. It is nice to get a reminder in the mail that your baby has moved to a new stage of development and helpful to get information on current ideas about child care. It may save you a trip to your baby reference book, or it may remind you to go on to the next section of that book. Each issue is full of ideas that will fit into all the categories of both record sheets. You can choose what you like and jot them down in the appropriate place. Another feature of *Growing Child* is that it recommends toys that are beneficial to babies and young children at different ages. You can send away for these toys that are often difficult to find in stores. See chapter 3 for more information, and note the contact information in the bibliography.

Another helpful guide to have is a landmark handbook published by the National Association for the Education of Young Children (NAEYC), called *Developmentally Appropriate Practices from Birth to Age 8*, Second Edition. It has the most current information about what are considered appropriate interactions for parents and caregivers of young children. The general information is helpful, and the specifics provide important guidelines. Refer to the bibliography.

Activities for Cognitive Development

Cognitive-development activities all have to do with learning. Any activity that you find that helps your child understand the world he lives in is a learning activity. You can introduce a learning activity at any time of day—simply explain all you can to your child and encourage him to see, hear, touch, taste, and smell all that comes his way. Providing this kind of exposure and guidance is natural for parents.

You will find activities with all the toys you make in this book to be excellent entries for this section. For example, if you make a Color Box, you could write as one entry, "Play with Color Box." (See page 103 for details about this activity.) This activity is designed specifically for cognitive development, but because the child manipulates the color objects as part of the activity, it also has a fine-motor component. Also, playing together with the box is social. Naming each object with the color word is a language-development exercise. Then, because there is skill development in all four of these areas, this activity offers self-confidence development as well.

Cognitive development goes on all the time. By virtue of whatever your child is experiencing, he is learning. You might be able to understand this by realizing that you too are learning all the time from each and every daily experience that you encounter. Because your child's brain grows rapidly in the early years, he is constantly learning. If he experiences a stimulating environment that is mostly positive, he will be learning at an optimal rate. If he mostly experiences a negative, nonstimulating environment, he will learn poor habits. You are the one who directs this continual learning process for your child and keeps it interesting for him by showing him how diverse the world is.

Activities for Motor Development

This area on the chart includes fine-motor or gross-motor activities. Fine-motor skills encompass movements in the hands. These break down into the pincer grasp (thumb and forefinger used to pick up small objects), wrist development, and a wide range of manipulative (handling) skills. Activities related to this area include doing puzzles, stringing beads, and writing. Clay or play-dough play provides children with a special opportunity for finger-muscle development and creative expression. Gross-motor skills encompass full-body movements such as rolling over, sitting, crawling, standing, walking, running, jumping, and hopping, which develop in a sequential order.

Activities for Fine-Motor Development

Play dough offers a fun and useful first activity in the fine-motor skills area. Encourage your child to form the clay or play dough into a ball by using a circular movement with the palm of the hand. Next, encourage pounding the ball into a pancake and then using the index finger to make two eyes, a nose, and a mouth. Your child will delight in this homemade happy face and probably will want to make quite a few more.

On another day, use the clay or play dough to roll out "snakes." Take a couple of spoonfuls of the dough and encourage your child to roll it back and forth on a tabletop to make a snake (or column of dough). Every child seems to want to do this instinctively with play dough. Once you have skinny snakes, they coil easily to form baskets or snails. Now you have another excellent fine-motor activity for your child—encouraging him to make a handle and fruit for the basket, or put eyes on his snail. As you can see, creativity is also part of this activity.

Fine-motor activities, such as playing with clay, also have links to other skill areas. Cognitive learning is served because the child learns more about texture when he plays with clay. When the child is old enough, he learns about parts making a whole as he participates in making play dough from scratch. When you play with your child as he plays with the dough, you further his social skills. Language skills are enhanced from the added talk that takes place as you play together and comment about what you are doing. The pride that comes with the accomplishment of making something out of the clay promotes a sense of self-esteem and confidence.

A classic fine-motor-development activity involves children spooning beans or rice from one bowl to another. In doing this activity, a child learns about the texture and weight of uncooked rice or beans. She might also be learning about counting if you decide to count each spoonful, and she will have an

Make Your Own Play Dough

Every child loves play dough. Use this recipe to make your own . . . in a color that matches your rug or floor, where at least some of it is likely to wind up!

1/2 cup salt
1 cup flour
2 tablespoons cream of tartar
1 cup water
1 tablespoon salad oil
food coloring (optional)

Mix together everything but food coloring in a saucepan. Cook over medium heat until it forms a ball, about three to five minutes. Mix in food coloring. Let mixture cool before giving it to your child.

enjoyable social interaction with you during this activity. Moreover, she will be exposed to language as you discuss how much of the rice or beans to put on each spoonful and how the transfer is being made from one bowl to the other. Self-confidence grows when your child enjoys the accomplishment of transferring the contents of one bowl directly to the other.

Here is a unique idea you will love. Have you ever heard of reflexology? It has been recognized for thousands of years by many civilizations. Today it is a science started at the turn of the twentieth century by Dr. William Fitzgerald, an American physician. Through his own experimentation he found that points in the hands and in the feet are directly related to important internal parts of the body. They are related in such a way that if massaged, they will enhance health in those areas of the body. For example, the fingers and the toes represent the brain, and the upper part of the palm and the ball of the foot represent the heart, lungs, and breast areas. All of the hand and all of the foot represent all of the body.

The lesson here is that the pleasant, natural, and bonding experience of massaging your child's hands and feet will at the same time improve his health. In addition, in the hand area you will also be stimulating fine-motor development. Sounds like hand and foot massages are a must. Although general movements over the whole area make good sense, you also have the opportunity to focus on a particular area that might be especially weak for your child. What a good idea to write down on your chart.

Activities for Gross-Motor Development

Gross-motor development concentrates on the development of the large-muscle groups, such as those involving arm, leg, and trunk movement. To begin with, you will gently move your baby's arms and legs into different positions, whether in the crib, to get ready for a bath, and so on. As you move your baby's arms and legs in different positions throughout the day, you can identify them as left and right. For example, as you put on a pair of pants, you can say as you pull each leg through, "Left foot, right foot." Putting on a shirt you can say, "Left hand, right hand." By repetition you will be teaching a concept that will be useful for a long time to come.

Another activity that relates to full-arm movement is crossing the midline of the body. (The midline of the body is an imaginary line that divides the body into right and left from head to toe.) This means that your child can use the right hand to reach for something on the left side of the body and the left hand to reach for something on the right side of the body. Most babies can do this when they are a few months old. Others with delayed development need encouragement and a little bit of help to do it. Just as crawling is known to be important to brain development because of the cross-patterning of the body, so is baby's ability to cross the midline of his body at a few months of age.

You can make a game out of "crossing the midline" that develops this skill once your child reaches the appropriate stage. Place an object on one side of your child's body, gently hold down the hand closest to it, and require him to cross the midline of his body to get it with the other hand. Do this on both sides for just a few seconds each time. This is also a good activity for a preschooler who shows no hand dominance and seems to pick things up with whichever hand is closest to the object. This will probably encourage left- or right-handedness if dominance in either hand is delayed. Being able to cross the midline of the body is necessary before children can learn to read and write, so this can serve as an enjoyable reading-and-writing readiness activity too.

A major cognitive experience here is the opportunity to learn "left" and "right." There is also great social interaction between parent and child. Language is a major part of this activity. Once again, self-confidence is the by-product of new learning.

Activities for Social Development

There is hardly a moment when your child will be truly alone during his youngest years. Social activities take place all day long. As your child learns, he finds himself in a relationship with whomever is doing the teaching—parent, grandparent, caregiver, or friend. As he learns to walk and master other developmental milestones, he will also be growing in relationships with others. Even as he takes a walk, the intent of the activity is really for sharing time together as you experience the beautiful outdoors with its fresh air and sunshine. All of your talking time builds language development. Through all your interactions with your child, you are giving a message about what you think of your child. What you think determines what your child will think of himself, his ultimate concept of self-confidence. Any play activity, daily ritual, or other interaction makes an appropriate entry for the social section of the chart.

Activities for Language Development

Language development plays a major part in all development (see the chart on page xv). As your child's caregiver, your language patterns have a direct influence on the quality of your child's self-expression. The language you speak will be the language your child speaks. Your grammar and sentence structure will have a major effect as well. Here's an idea: Add a word or phrase to whatever language your child already has. For example, if your child speaks in one-word sentences, say them back to your child as two. For example, turn "Car" into "Blue car" and "Truck" into "Big truck." If your child is speaking in two-word sentences, say them back to your child as three. "Blue car" can become "Big blue car" and "Big truck" can be "Big noisy truck." As you add words, you add important information. "The ball" can become "Bounce the ball." "Bounce the ball" can become "Bounce the ball well." There are no rules for this activity. The idea is to encourage conversation. With conversation comes language development. Let it flow naturally.

Language activity shows its connection with the other developmental areas in lots of ways. Your child's cognitive development flourishes as you speak to him. Much of what you say is in the form of giving directions, and many times these directions involve asking your child to use her motor skills, stimulating development in that area. "Bounce the ball" is a good example. Because you don't usually speak unless there is someone to hear you, social development is another typical component of language activities. Watch your child's sense of self-confidence grow as you communicate with her and express interest in everything she does!

Consider taking language development to the next level with storytelling. You might try telling "The Story of the Day" when you put your child to bed. Everyone likes stories, and who would not want to hear one about oneself? Start from the beginning and tell your child what happened throughout the day, starting from morning and ending with hearing this very story. This activity is also stimulating for the mind and memory (cognitive skills!). As understanding of language begins to grow, your child will be able to participate in this activity, recalling the events of the day along with you. You might want to begin the story in the same way each night. The familiarity can provide a welcome sense of security to the child. It can also be an occasion to repeat any concepts you would like your child to remember. For example, "This is the story of the day of _____ whose address is _____ and whose telephone number is _____." You can add your child's birth date, $1 + 1 = 2$, or whatever you would like to teach. Cognitive learning is built into the story. Motor development could be added by putting in a hand motion, such as a small wave "hello" and "good-bye" to visitors you saw that day. Social activity comes from building the story together. Self-confidence is very high in this case. A story that is about your child and his activities focuses positive attention on him.

"Baby's First Poem" and "Play and Say" are activities you also might want to list in the Language category of your Record Sheet. They are fun to say and require both you and your baby to participate. The first activity is designed to encourage physical action and the second is to encourage language response. The poems support learning in the cognitive area. They are filled with fine-motor activities. Because of the interaction they encourage between parent and child, they could not be more social. Moreover, all the focus on your child will greatly enhance self-confidence. The text for the poems follows.

Baby's First Poem

Objective: To provide an interaction for parent and baby centered around the things baby can do or is learning to do during his first year of life.

Description: This is a poem about the first physical movements babies learn how to make. As you say the words, do the motions gently with your baby.

One plus one equals two. (Show with your fingers.)
Two plus two equals four.
Right now I don't know any more.
I can stand up. (Move baby up.)
I can sit down. (Move baby down.)
I can move my whole self all around. (Move baby gently in a small circle.)
I can raise my right hand. (Raise baby's right hand.)
I can raise my left hand too. (Raise baby's left hand.)
That's not all that I can do!
I can raise my right foot. (Raise baby's right foot.)
I can raise my left foot. (Raise baby's left foot.)
I can touch my toes, (Touch baby's toes.)
And I can touch my nose. (Touch baby's nose.)
I can clap my hands, (Clap baby's hands.)
Pat my head, (Pat baby's head.)
Cover my eyes, (Cover baby's eyes.)
And play peek-a-boo. (Uncover baby's eyes.)
That's a lot that I can do!
I wave "Hi," (Direct baby's hands.)
But now I say, "Bye-bye." (Direct baby's hands.)

Play and Say

Objective: To stimulate and encourage toddlers to talk. Because the poem asks questions, the child will enjoy through rhyme his own parts for participation.

   Description: Poem with parts for child participation to promote language development.

   Dramatize any parts you wish with hand motions.

What is your name?
How old are you?
Glad to meet you.
Yes, it's true.
Let's play a game that's fun to do!
Listen to the words I choose, and tell me what it is you use.
What do you drink from? (Child responds to this question and
those that follow.)
What do you eat with?
What is the food on?
What do you like to eat?
What do you like to drink?
What do you like to play?
And what do you like to say?

Activities for Self-Confidence

Self-confidence development is a summative, more global area. Referring to the diagram "The picture of development" in the introduction, you can see that self-confidence is the seal that develops from mastering skills and having abilities. Help your child to thrive in all areas. In addition, add respect and appreciation. A significant way to show your child respect is to say "please" when you ask her to do something for you. An important way to show appreciation is to say "thank you" after he does what you asked, or did something positive on his own. The way to teach your child to say "please" and "thank you" is to say "please" and "thank you" to your child. Communicate uniqueness to your child. Help him to understand he is special and that you value his special qualities. Don't forget about directing his behavior. Change the word "misbehavior" to "mistaken behavior." Then follow through with teaching your child how not to make the same mistake again.

5

Collecting Daily Tips

The Daily Schedule

Running a household is a lot like running a business, with an important segment of that business devoted to taking care of your child. He needs a full program of care, from the minute he wakes up in the morning to the moment he goes to sleep at night. Since this care is mixed in with other aspects of the business, it can be complicated to keep everything running smoothly. A memory and planning aid like Record Sheet 2 can be helpful.

This record-keeping worksheet is a place for jotting down activities that are related to daily schedules you have with your child, such as mealtimes, bathing, walks, and so on. It is a good place to collect ideas that will make your day run more smoothly with your child. Find a reproducible copy of this sheet in Appendix B. Make a few copies at a time so that each week you can make a new program to follow.

Nutrition Ideas

Nutrition for today's children is in crisis. Children are routinely offered too much food, and also too much food of poor nutritional quality, such as fast food. Many children eat lots of sweets and fried foods that are low in nutrients and too little fruits, vegetables, and whole grains that are high in nutrients. Eating should not be treated like a form of entertainment. Keeping that in mind, it should be easier for you to select and prepare food for your child. Dining is a style of eating that should be taught along with eating. It includes specific table protocol and the art of conversation. It is pleasurable just as entertainment is, but it is not entertainment. It is a full activity that is stimulating and enriching, an entire eating process all of its own.

Here are some hints that you might find helpful as you teach your child how to eat properly, enjoy eating, and obtain proper nourishment.

1. Use the food pyramid designed by the U.S. Department of Agriculture to determine how many servings a day from each food group you should serve your child.
   a. Serve your child six to eleven servings of whole grains a day. Whole-grain foods are natural cereals, rice, pasta, and breads made with no preservatives, artificial colors, or flavors.
   b. Next serve three to five servings a day of vegetables.
   c. Be sure to serve two to four servings a day of fruits.
   d. If you want to include meat, fish, and poultry in the diet, limit them to two to three servings.
   e. If you want to include dairy products, again limit them to two or three servings.
   f. Serve fats, oils, and sweets sparingly. Think of fats in terms of a tablespoon of butter or mayonnaise. Think of oils as unsaturated like safflower or corn. Think of sweets as those that are freshly made, not processed.

2. Estimate your number of servings by thinking of a serving size as the size of your child's fist.

3. Serve water to your child all day long, always from a cup, beginning at around three months of age.

4. Serve fruits as much as possible instead of fruit juice. Serve juice only when it is freshly made.

5. Teach your child to eat slowly and to chew the food thoroughly. This will help to reduce total food consumption and will increase the digestibility of the foods eaten.

6. Serve meals in a relaxed atmosphere without excess noise, stress, and emotional reactivity.

7. Breast-feeding is ideal for the first year. Mashed banana is a wonderful first food that you can introduce anytime from six months of age or older.

8. Formula given in a bottle is a substitute for breast-feeding. Water and juice should be given in a cup. No other drinks are appropriate for children. Avoid drinks that have any artificial ingredients.

Ideas for Rest and Sleep

Rest and sleep are as important to excellent health as nutrition and exercise. The human body was meant to sleep for long hours. Nature designed this process to be coordinated with darkness. Growing out of this concept comes the idea of a regular sleep schedule. Young children need extra hours of sleep that they get in the form of naps. Besides the value of sleep to the health of the body, sleep separates days and makes each one a new adventure with a fresh start.

The adult sleep requirement has been reduced from ten to twelve hours to about eight. This is not because the human body has changed. It is because society has changed. As life started becoming easier in terms of physical activity, less sleep was required to accomplish the necessary rest and body repair. In addition, as times became more complicated, the amount of work and things to do increased, requiring people to stay up later to do them. The discovery of electricity fit right in, giving people artificial light for doing activities during the nighttime hours.

Although newborns sleep most of the time, they settle out in the toddler and twos stages to about twelve to thirteen hours. Then childhood sleep is reduced once again from twelve hours to about ten. The reduction once again comes about more from the change in lifestyle, busier, less physical, and more complicated, than from a decreased need of the human body.

Similar to the way your child should eat until he is full, so he should sleep until he wakes up. This should be a natural process. Eating enough nutrients will guide his feeling of being full, and so will his sleep guide his feeling of being rested. Just as we have designed a three-meal-a-day and two- to three-snack schedule for eating, so we have designed a ten- to twelve-hour block of time for sleeping that includes naps.

Meals and nutrition vary each day because of schedules, and so it is with sleep. Although schedules should be set up to follow a basic pattern, it is okay to have the concept of flexibility that works with different kinds of daily activities. The routine is important as a way to ensure positive health practices, but it need not be rigid.

A major role of sleep is body cell repair. Adequate sleep has a direct effect on the entire functioning of the body. One way you can see it is with your child's mood. With enough sleep, your child will have more pleasant cooperative moods and also be able to function at his best.

Sleep, like food, is not something to take lightly. Deprivation takes a specific toll on your child's health. Sleep research tells us that it increases muscular and joint pain, magnifies the negative consequences of stress, and promotes insulin resistance, abnormal blood sugar regulation, and weight gain.

Here are some helpful hints to help you monitor and carry out an effective sleep and rest routine with your child.

1. Give your child a bath at night. This begins the relaxation process.
2. Plan quiet activities after dinner to begin the winding down process.
3. Set up the sleep environment to be cool, dark, and quiet.
4. Play soft music for your child to help him fall asleep.
5. Be firm about a regular bedtime for your child. This will train his biological clock to help him be sleepy at bedtime and feel like getting up when it is morning.
6. Keep all caffeine away from your child. Coffee, which is a stimulant that suppresses sleep, can stay in the circulatory system for up to fourteen hours. Many sodas and chocolate have caffeine in them as well.
7. Set up a regular schedule of checking on your child while he is asleep. Start by checking every fifteen minutes and then lengthen the intervals. This gives security in a positive way and is not related to your child's crying to call for your attention.
8. Hold and rock your baby as much as you want. Have your baby sleep near to you if you want. Because modern society is so complicated, let nature guide you as you make bedtime into the wonderful relaxing time it should be.

Ideas for Self-Help

Self-help is a category that describes taking care of oneself and one's belongings. It leads to activities like dressing and putting things away. It is closely related to the development of independence, a gradual process that takes place from infancy through about age eighteen. Certain ages represent milestone passages in this area. The first one is at two years of age, the time your toddler will begin to see himself as an entity independent of you. The next one is at five years old, at kindergarten, and the official time for making friends and relating to them in a personal and meaningful way. After that is puberty, a transition time into the teenage years. As he did when he was two years old, your child will in a different way see himself as an entity independent of you—able to make independent decisions and form strong personal peer friendships on a new level. The last stage, at eighteen, is the time for mature independence and a true ability to make appropriate decisions and meaningful friendships.

Before your toddler is ready to start picking up and putting away toys at around three years of age, you can begin a readiness game. Mark a large circle on a toy shelf—it could be on paper that is taped to the shelf or a chalk circle. Place an easy-to-handle toy on the circle. With your child watching, take the toy off its circle. Give your child the toy and ask him to return it to its proper place. In this way you send the message that everything has its proper place, but you are restricting the activity to only one item that your child can learn to handle successfully. Repeat the game as often as you and your child continue to find it fun. When you notice success with one toy, you can expand the game to two items and then three or four. When you notice that your child handles several items in this way successfully, he is ready to go on to the next stage.

This is the time to teach your child how to pick up and put away his toys as a regular activity after playing with them. A good way to introduce this activity is to pitch in and help. Remember that what may look like a little mess to an adult can represent a confusing sorting task for a tot. It helps if you alternate putting away toys with your child until everything is picked up. Your friendly participation will encourage your child to have a pleasant attitude toward cleaning up. Once you see that your child has the hang of this activity, you can move on once again.

The follow-up to sharing the clean-up activity is to say something like, "You can't put all those toys away by yourself." When your child is ready, the welcome reply will probably be, "Oh, yes I can. Want to see?"

Ideas for Play

Play is a child's work, and toys are your child's tools. True play is an open-ended learning experience. It may sound frivolous, but play is an extremely valuable activity for your child. With curiosity at the helm, your child through play will learn myriad basic concepts—heavy and light, big and little, rough and smooth, open and shut, in and out, and many others. As you will see from the toys you can make from directions in this book, play can also teach self-awareness, colors, letters, numbers, shapes, and reading.

The most formed the toy, the least value it has, and the least formed the toy, the most value it has. Most formed refers to a toy that does one thing. For example, you press one button down, and one figure pops up. Least formed refers to items and materials like sand, water, clay and play dough, bubbles, dolls, pegs and pegboards, balls, blocks, and other items for creative endeavors.

Play should also be with toys that have play value. Play value is encompassed in those qualities that invite you to play. The most beautiful or expensive toy is of no value if nobody wants to play with it. The qualities that seem to attract children to play with toys include something

- interesting to see
- interesting to touch

- that requires interaction
  with the toy
  with others and the toy
- with surprise

Toys high in play value do not have to be expensive. They do not have to be complicated. They do not have to be store-bought. As a matter of fact, they do not have to be any special thing at all! An example is a washcloth. Many a parent throughout the generations has used washcloths to play peek-a-boo. Probably every parent has their own approach, but basically the game is to cover your face with the washcloth, remove it, and then say, "peek-a-boo!" Check out the humble washcloth for the above characteristics. It has every single one of them.

As you make the toys in this book, you will see that they all have high play value. They are all simple, easy to make, and inexpensive. As you will discover, most of them are made from common materials, such as index cards and paper, simple folders, and plastic containers. Your recycle bin will become an endless supply of raw materials for creating new and different toys.

Miscellaneous Ideas

Once you start asking for parenting tips, you may find it hard to keep up with all of the good ideas people tell you. Although some advice may fit into neat categories, other suggestions will not. Whether you have an abundance of suggestions or a lot of hard-to-classify tips, use a "Miscellaneous" record sheet to organize them so you can find them again later. Here's an example of a classic "miscellaneous" tip: Your neighbor tells you that when she had very small children, they became upset whenever she left the room. To keep them from crying, she made a game out of her comings and goings. She would tell her children: "I'm going away, but I'm going to surprise you." When she popped in on her children from time to time, she surprised them with, "Peek-a-boo, I see you!"

At first glance this wonderful tip appears to belong with self-help ideas, because the woman's children were younger than two years old and naturally had a strong attachment to her. Being attached to someone who goes away brings discomfort. However, on second look, this activity does not really promote self-help because it doesn't result in helping the children truly develop independence from their mother. The toddlers in this case are not actively trying to accomplish a new task.

You might think this activity is about play instead, because it is a creative version of the old game "peek-a-boo." However, in this case the purpose of the activity is not to play, nor does it include specific information about toys and play. The element of playful surprise is just a by-product of one mother's inventive idea for leaving her children's room without making them cry. Miscellaneous turns out to be a wonderful category for gathering just this kind of useful but hard-to-name information.

The simplest suggestion can end up making an enormous difference, so it's worth trying all those that you hear about that appeal to you. Some suggestions are so simple that they take no extra time at all. As you take care of your child, you may find it easy and helpful to say or do one new thing at a time. Whether you want to implement one helpful hint or a major new program, rely on Record Sheet 2 to help you as you navigate the interesting, exciting, and rewarding world of parenting.

Part TWO

Making Your Own
Educational Toys

6

Making and Using
Successful Toys

Making the Toys

Successful toys for infants and toddlers are those that both of
you like. If *you* like them, you will automatically present
them in an interesting way to your child. Bright colors, a
"peek-a-boo" concealed part, a pleasant sound, an appealing
texture, or a pleasant taste or smell are all important qualities. You and your baby will be partners when it comes to
making your toys come alive. As you get to know your own
baby, you will learn what delights him. He will have his own
way of leading you toward making his perfect toy. If you have
the desire, you definitely will have the ability to put together
homemade educational toys that your child will love.

Once you start, you will see that toy making has nothing to do with being an artist or an educator. The materials are few, the methods are short, and the finished products reflect simplicity. If you know how to cut and paste, you are ready to go!

Although these toys are meant to accomplish certain objectives and not to excel in beauty and design, you will see that they are all intrinsically attractive. Just follow the directions and you and your baby will be delighted with the results. If you are talented in art, you will have the opportunity to make each project as unique and elaborate as you wish.

Homemade Books.   The toy projects include instructions for many different kinds of homemade books. Construction-paper pages are pretty and easy for babies to handle. Because they rip easily, however, protect them with clear contact paper or by laminating. You can also increase durability by making pages from lightweight cardboard, tagboard (also called oak tag), or large index cards, which are firmer. You can even create books from ready-made photo albums; make your own labels to add words to your books. Felt is another wonderful medium for making books because it adds the quality of texture.

Element of Surprise.   An element of surprise is always good to build into a toy. For example, you can add a page with a flap to a Color Book. If you put your child's name or something like "peek-a-boo" or "Surprise!" under the flap, watch how delighted your child will be! You will find that adding personal surprises to your toys will be as much fun for you as it will be for your child. What's more, your delight with the toys you make will enhance your play experience with your child. Your positive interaction with your child and his toys will be as important to the success of the toys as the toys themselves.

Selecting Materials

In Part 2 of this book you will learn to make toys in each of the six learning categories. Each of the six learning categories has its own chapter, starting with Chapter 7, and each chapter has suggestions for making a number of toys that can enhance learning in that category, for example, shapes. Each set of toy-making instructions includes a list of the materials needed to make the toy. The suggested materials are readily available to most people.

Substitutions Are Okay!   It's perfectly okay to make substitutions if you think they would work just as well or better. For example, you might choose to use crayons instead of markers and double-stick tape instead of white glue or paste. I list index cards in a recommended size for many projects, but often other sizes would work also.

Clear Contact Paper.   I like to use clear contact paper on toys I make and I mention it frequently in this book. You can find clear contact paper on rolls in most hardware stores, supermarkets, or discount stores. Once you have cut the size you need, peel off a little of the paper backing and stick the clear side onto your toy. Then roll away the rest of the paper backing as you continue to apply the clear side to the toy surface. This method is a practical way to decrease the amount of bubbles you will get on your paper.

Lamination.   For many of the toys in this book, I suggest laminating to protect either the toy or your child. Lamination services are conveniently available at most office supply stores.

Oak Tag.   Oak tag, also called tagboard, usually comes in large sheets of different sizes, and you might have to cut them to a more usable size. If you have difficulty finding any of the materials, remember to look for satisfactory substitutes. Different parts of the country have different resources.

Safety

Whatever materials you choose, make sure they are safe for children. Because aluminum foil and some wrapping paper can contain lead, be sure to cover these materials with clear contact paper; after all, most babies will put everything they can in their mouth! Check any plastic containers you are using often. They split easily and those edges can be sharp. After you have considered and taken care of the safety aspect, the sky is the limit as you make your toys. The ideas presented here are basic and designed to get you off to a good start making your own individualized, creative toys.

Using the Toys

These toys are designed for play that is exploratory, open-ended, and fun.

Just as there is no end to the creativity you can put into your toys, there is no end to the number of ways you and your baby will think up to play with them. Remember, these are toys, and that means they are for play. They are not curriculum materials designed for drill and practice or anything like that. These toys are designed for play that is exploratory, open-ended, and fun. There are really no exceptions.

7

Toys About Self-Awareness

Developing Self-Awareness

A baby's sight develops gradually, becoming refined over time. As his vision improves, so does his appreciation of the world he sees. At four weeks, your baby already takes an interest in faces that are close to his, about eight inches away. By the time he is eight weeks old, you will notice that your baby enjoys seeing people move about the room. As time goes by, your baby gains more opportunities to notice the people around him and to look at his own image in a mirror. He will be getting to know his house and all the things in it. Little by little, your baby is making connections that will lead to a recognition of himself and of his family. Your baby at eight weeks is busy developing a sense of self-awareness.

It takes a full three years for your baby to achieve a developed sense of self-awareness. You play a major role in your baby's gradual process of self-discovery. Your major contribution is simply to be there for him as much as possible and to provide as much approval and positive feedback as possible. The toys in this section are specifically designed to help you interact with your baby in a fun and positive way. These toys have the capacity to foster your child's self-awareness and the growing independence that goes along with it. The toys are My Name Toy, My Family, My Story, My Friends, Personalized Room Deco, Mirror-Mirror, Shoe Bag, and Toy Bag.

My Name Toy

FIGURE 7.1   My Name Toy

Age Range: Birth to Eighteen Months

Objective: To teach your baby visual recognition of his name as a word and visual recognition of his image as a picture. With this toy, he will learn gradually that both are ways of representing himself.

Description: A stand-up card with your baby's name on one side and a corresponding picture of him on the other—two ways of teaching your child to recognize his own name.

Materials:

- One photograph of your baby
- Two five-by-eight-inch unlined index cards

- Clear contact paper
- Cellophane tape
- White glue, paste, or double-stick tape
- Scissors
- Markers or crayons

Directions: Print your child's name on one side of one index card. Begin with a capital letter and write the rest in lowercase letters. Write clearly, in large letters. Attach a picture of your child to the other card. Tape the cards across the top back to back so that the tape will not show. Then cover both cards together with clear contact paper or laminate them to make one My Name Toy. This protection will keep the picture from tearing and the name from smearing. Then fold the two cards.

How to Use and Enjoy This Toy

Babies like cards *and* attractive pictures, and you are providing both in a high-interest, durable picture with this toy. Whichever side your baby sees, comment on it and call it by your child's name.

Birth to Three Years.   In the first few months your baby will simply look at the card while you hold it. Soon she will be able to hold it herself, and turn it over to look at both sides. Before long she will carry it around with her and show it to family members and friends, inviting them to look at it and pointing out her own name and picture.

My Family

Age Range: Birth to Three Years

Objective: To help your child learn by name all the people in his family. In addition, this toy is designed to teach the concept of "family."

Description: This is a homemade book made from a photo album with the title "My Family." I recommend placing all photos on right-hand pages and all labels, written with a marker, on index cards fastened to left-hand pages. For each picture, place a label that names the family member on the opposite side of the page. For example, you might have a photo of Grandma on one right-hand page, and a label reading "Grandma" on the left-hand page opposite the photograph. Show each family member individually. Include whoever is in the family, such as Mommy, Daddy, Grandma, Grandpa, child, brother, sister, cousins, aunt, and uncle. Identify brothers, sisters, cousins, aunts, and uncles by their names (for example, "Aunt Irene"; "Cindy" for a sister named Cindy; "Nana" for a grandmother, if she goes by that name). Not only a photo book, this is also a beginning reading book.

To be in *this* book, you have to be in the family! Because the book is about family members, it will be of very high interest to your baby; he will want to look at it over and over. From his earliest days, your child will gain familiarity with the people in his family and the words that represent them.

Materials:

- Photo album
- Four-by-six-inch index cards, as many as there are members of your family or pages in your photo album
- Sharply focused, individual photographs of each member of the family
- Marker or crayon

Directions: Print the name of each family member in large letters (capital and lowercase) on each index card. Center each card on the left-hand page across from the matching photograph attached on the right-hand page. Write the words "My Family" on an index card for the title page.

When placing the photographs in the photo album, standardize the way you mount the photos in the book. If most of the photographs are framed to be mounted vertically and you have a few that are horizontal, trim the horizontal photos to fit a vertical mounting scheme. If most of the photographs are horizontal and you have a few that are vertical, trim the vertical photos to fit on the horizontal pages.

Using a marker or crayon, clearly print each name on an index card. Center the label on the left-hand page across from the photograph it refers to. Mount the labels and the photographs in a standard way so the label pages and the photo pages maintain a consistent look throughout the book.

How to Use and Enjoy This Toy

Birth to Eighteen Months.   Look through the book with your baby or toddler. For each family member in the book, point to the label on the left-hand page and read the family member's name. Then point to the photo on each right-hand page and repeat the person's name. This process over time teaches your child that a particular word and its corresponding picture are both ways to represent the real person. Your baby or toddler will love looking at the pictures of his favorite people and will soon enjoy naming them too. This is a nice way for everyone in the family to enjoy family pictures with your child. It is also a good way to remind your baby or toddler of Grandma or Grandpa or other family members who might be far away.

Eighteen Months to Three Years.   Just as with your infant, go through the book. Point out to your child and read a family member's name from the left-hand page. Then point to that person's photograph on the right-hand page and repeat his name. By repetition and growing familiarity with this toy, your child will gradually learn to read this book on his own. At first, you can read aloud all the names; gradually, however, let your child say more and more of the names as you simply point to them. Soon your child will be able to read every label.

After your child has mastered this version of the game, cover up the pictures and let your child read the words only. In time you can phase yourself out of the process completely—just sit back, relax, and enjoy seeing your child read My *Family* all by himself!

My Story

FIGURE 7.2   My Story

FIGURE 7.3   My Story

Age Range: Birth to Three Years

Objective: To help your child see himself as part of positive past experiences. In addition, the toy is designed to provide a high-interest story.

Description: This is a homemade book with the title "My Story." I recommend placing photos on the right-hand pages and word labels written with a marker on index cards on all the left-hand pages. For each picture, place a card with the appropriate number of words (depending on child's age) on the corresponding left-hand page.

Use any photographs for this book that relate to your child. They might show places he has gone, pictures of his home, or the people or things in his home. They might relate to a certain theme, such as snapshots from a family trip or his birthday party.

Add words to go with these photographs that reflect your child's own language level—in general, one word for children up to one year old, two words for children up to two years old, and three words for children up to three years old. This book is both a picture *and* a reading book. Because the book is about what your child knows or has experienced, it will hold a lot of interest for him; your child will want to look at it repeatedly. By repetition and a growing familiarity with this book, your child will form positive associations with the people, places, and things that are meaningful to him, as well as the words that represent them.

When Writing Labels . . .

In general, use one word for children up to one year old, two words for children up to two years old, and three words for children up to three years old.

Materials:

- Photo album
- Four-by-six-inch index cards, as many as there are pages in the photo album
- Photographs of people, places, or things familiar to your child
- Marker or crayon

Directions: Collect the photographs that you would like to include in this book. Put the photographs in order if you like.

For each photograph, create a label: On an index card, use the marker or crayon to print an appropriate descriptive word or words in large letters. Use a capital initial letter, followed by lowercase letters, as in "Home." Trim all cards to the same dimensions, and use a consistent printing style. Center and attach each card on a left-hand page of the photo album, to appear opposite the photograph it describes.

Write the words "My Story" on an index card for the title page (the first page of the book).

Mount each photograph in the photo album on a right-hand page, one photograph per page. Center each photograph on the page. Make sure all photographs in the album are mounted either vertically or horizontally for consistency. For example, if most of your photographs are vertical shots and you have a few photos to include that are horizontal, trim the horizontal images to create a vertical presentation.

How to Use and Enjoy This Toy

Birth to Eighteen Months.   Read the book with your baby or toddler. Point to each left-hand page and read the word or words there. Then point to each right-hand page and repeat the words as you look at the photograph. This process teaches your child that a particular word and its corresponding picture are different ways to represent the same thing. (For example, one card-and-picture combination might both be identified as "The park.") Your baby or toddler will love looking at the pictures and will soon enjoy participating in saying the words just as you have been saying them. This is a nice way for everyone to enjoy family pictures with your child and also a good way to remind your baby or toddler of past pleasant experiences.

Eighteen Months to Three Years.   Read through the book with your toddler, enjoying every photograph. Point to the left-hand page and read the words there. Then point to the photograph across the page on the right-hand side and repeat the words to your child as you look at the picture. By repetition and familiarity your child will gradually learn to read this book on his own. Say all the words yourself at first, but gradually let your child try saying them as you point them out. Soon your child will be able to read the words as you point to them.

After that, make a new game in which you cover the pictures and let your child read the words alone. In time you will be able to phase yourself out of the game entirely. You can sit back, relax, and enjoy hearing your child read "My Story" all by himself.

The "My Story" Library?

Once you make one "My Story" book, you will probably enjoy making *many* more, each emphasizing a different theme or event. Whenever you have a roll of film developed, have two sets of images made instead of one. You can send some of these duplicate photographs to others, but you might reserve certain images to use in these very special, very popular "My Story" books for your child.

My Friends

Age Range: Birth to Three Years

Objective: To help your child see himself as part of a group of friends. In addition, this toy is designed to introduce your child to new high-interest vocabulary words—the names of his friends.

Description: This special homemade book with the title "My Friends" is reserved for pictures of your child's playmates. In a four-by-six-inch photo album, or whatever size album you prefer, individual photographs of your child's friends are placed on right-hand pages, and labels identifying the friends by name are placed on left-hand pages opposite their photos.

The photographs in this book are limited to your child's friends. You may have many pictures of your child's friends already, or you may need to ask the children's parents for pictures that you can include in this book. Now you have another book that your child will be fascinated by and that will teach him new vocabulary as a bonus.

Be sure to choose words to accompany these pictures that are appropriate for your child's language level—use just one word as a label for children up to one year old, two-word pairs for children up to two years old, and three-word phrases for children up to three years old. "My Friends" is a picture book *and* a reading book. Because the book is about children your child knows, it will be of high interest to him; be prepared for your child to want to read it again and again!

Materials:

- Photo album
- Four-by-six-inch index cards (as many cards as there are pages in the photo album)
- Photographs of your child's friends
- Marker or crayon

Directions: Collect photographs of your child's playmates. Arrange the photographs in a certain order if you wish.

Mount each photograph in the photo album on a right-hand page, one photograph per page. Center each photograph on the page. Make sure all photographs in the album are mounted either vertically or horizontally for consistency. For example, if most of your photographs are vertical shots and you have a few photos to include that are horizontal, trim the horizontal images to create a vertical look for the image.

For each photograph, create a one-word, two-word, or three-word label, depending on your child's age. Trim all cards to the same dimensions. On an index card, use the marker or crayon to print an appropriate descriptive word or words in large letters. Use a capital initial letter followed by lowercase letters, as in "Joe" or "Joe smiles." Use a consistent printing style for all the labels. Center and attach each label on a left-hand page of the photo album, to appear opposite the photograph it describes.

Write the words "My Friends" on an index card for the title page (the first page of the book).

How to Use and Enjoy This Toy

Birth to Eighteen Months.   Read this book with your baby or toddler held close. Starting with a left-hand page, point to the page and read aloud the name printed there. Then point to the photograph on the corresponding right-hand page and repeat the name. This process teaches your child that a particular word and its corresponding picture are different ways to represent the same thing. For example, one card-and-picture combination might be "Cara," with "Cara" spelled out on one page and a photograph of Cara appearing on the opposite page. Your baby or toddler will love looking at the photographs and will soon enjoy participating in saying the words just as you have been saying them. This is a nice way for everyone to enjoy friends' pictures with your child and also a good way to teach your child that he is part of another social group called "friends."

Eighteen Months to Three Years.   Read through the book with your child. Starting on the left-hand page, point to the label and read the word or words printed there. Then point to the photograph on the opposite page and repeat the words. By playing this game with your child, your child will be able to read this book on his own in time. As your child becomes familiar with the words and pictures, let him begin to say the words for himself, while you point them out. Soon you can simply point to the names and listen as your child reads them by himself. Now create a new game in which you cover the pictures and let your child read the names. Eventually your "job" will be to simply sit back, relax, and enjoy seeing your child read "My Friends" all by himself.

Make More Books!

After you and your child enjoy reading this book about "My Friends," you may want to branch out and make other simple books on topics of special interest to your child. You might make books about subjects such as "My Toys," "Flowers," "Trees," "Animals," and more. Just collect photographs or pictures from magazines that suit your chosen theme and follow the instructions as you did to make the "My Friends" book. There is no limit to the kinds of appealing books you can make or to the creativity you can put into these appealing projects.

Personalized Room Deco

FIGURE 7.4   Personalized Room Deco

Age Range: Birth to Three Years

Objective: To teach your child word recognition of his name and to associate it with his picture. It is also designed to help your child see how he has grown from an infant to a toddler to a two-year-old—and what he was like at many of the different stages in between.

Description: Personalized Room Deco is a colorful wall hanging with your child's name printed in large letters and a place for his picture. Just as your child will become familiar over time with the many other pictures and wall hangings in his house, so he will get to know this special one that will help him learn his own name.

Materials:

- Twelve-by-eighteen-inch oak tag board or open file folder
- Current photograph of your child
- Decorative ribbon
- Fabric scraps, wallpaper scraps, or wrapping-paper scraps
- Hole punch
- String or yarn, about two feet long
- Scissors
- White glue, paste, or double-stick tape
- Marker or crayon

Directions: Print your child's name in large letters on the oak tag or open folder, using markers or crayon. Begin with a capital letter and write the rest of the letters in lowercase. Make your child's name big, bold, and easy to read.

Make four photo corners out of ribbon and attach them to the center of the oak tag or folder, according to the dimensions of your child's photo. Place the photograph in the photo corners to hold it. Change photos as your child grows so they are always current. Instead of discarding or putting away old photos, however, place each new photo on top of the previous one. This provides a sequenced collection of photos that show how your baby is changing from babyhood up to three years of age.

Use more ribbon to print your child's name; attach to the hanging with glue or paste. (Wrapping yarn or felt is also nice to use to print your child's name and makes it stand out.) Use fabric scraps, wallpaper scraps, or wrapping-paper scraps to make a border around the hanging and to embellish the decorative look. There is no one way to do this—the more creativity you use, the better! After you have finished decorating the hanging, punch a hole in each of the top corners. Tie a string or yarn through the holes and display the finished product in a prominent spot on a wall in your child's room.

How to Use and Enjoy This Toy

Birth to Eighteen Months.   As you lift your baby out of the crib or greet your toddler in his bed first thing in the morning, carry him over to Personalized Room Deco, point to his name and say it, then point to his picture and repeat his name once more. In this way your child learns that the word for the name and the word for the picture are the same.

Eighteen Months to Three Years.   Every morning or evening, take your child over to his Personalized Room Deco. Point to his name, say it, and then point to the picture and say his name again. Occasionally, remove the photograph from the frame along with all the previous photos that are stored behind it. Place them on a table in sequence to show your child from youngest to oldest in the photos. Point to each picture in order and show your child how he has grown from a small baby to the big child he is today. As time goes on, let your child participate as much as possible in putting the photographs in sequential order.

Mirror, Mirror

FIGURE 7.5   Mirror Magic!

FIGURE 7.6   Unbreakable Mirror

Age Range: Birth to Three Years

Objective: To provide your child with the opportunity to use his reflected image as a stimulus to cognitive, social, and language growth.

Description: A mirror for play. You may use a large mirror hanging on a wall or a small handheld, unbreakable mirror that your child can manipulate.

Materials:

- A hanging wall mirror or an unbreakable toy mirror

Directions: Use a mirror that is already hanging somewhere in your house or buy an unbreakable mirror.

How to Use and Enjoy This Toy

Birth to Eighteen Months.   Show your baby his image in a mirror. Just have fun with this experience and see what happens. Let your baby be the guide. As he looks in the mirror and responds to his image, his expression will change. As he changes his expression, he will respond to his image again, as though it were a new image. You may notice this sequence take place over and over. This simple play activity helps your baby get to know himself better and better.

Eighteen Months to Three Years.   Continue with the free-form activity described for babies up to eighteen months old. Now add more specific exercises to the play. As you hold your toddler or two-year-old around the waist in front of a mirror, notice how he reaches out to the image in the mirror. If *you* make a gesture in the mirror, such as waving or smiling, your child will wave or smile back. If *you* make sounds, like click-click-click or la-la-la, your child probably will make those same sounds back, or try. If you see your child make a gesture or a sound, feel free to imitate it in response; also, encourage your child to make more gestures and sounds.

Toy Barn

FIGURE 7.7   Toy Barn

Age Range: Birth to Three Years

Objective: To help your baby develop independence, and to teach your child where things belong so that soon he will be able to participate in putting away his own belongings.

Description: The toy barn is really a child's shoe bag. Be sure the shoe pockets are large enough for the child to put toys into and pull toys out of the pockets easily.

Assign each toy a certain pocket in the shoe bag, and keep the assigned toy only in that particular pocket. With this easy-to-use bag, your child will learn to find his playthings. He will begin to learn a sense of order and of taking care of belongings.

Materials:

- A child's shoe bag, available at most baby supply stores
- Short strings, yarn, or ribbon to attach the shoe bag to a background
- Several soft toys that are at least the size of your fist

Directions: Attach the shoe bag with the short strings to a crib, playpen, door, or wall.

How to Use and Enjoy This Toy

Birth to Nine Months.   Place a soft toy in each pocket of the Toy Barn (shoe bag). The bag decorates the crib while neatly holding the soft toys. Each night, collect the toys from where they have been scattered in the crib and put them away in the pockets. Then pull them out and put them back in the crib for play the following morning.

Nine Months to Eighteen Months.   Place one of your child's favorite soft toys in each pocket of the Toy Barn. Whether in the crib, playpen, or some other location, put all the toys away at night in their pockets and watch your baby take them out in the morning. If you use the Toy Barn in the crib, you will be able to sleep a little later in the morning because your baby will have learned to find his own toys for play.

Eighteen Months to Three Years.   Place a soft toy in each pocket of the Toy Barn. Hang the Toy Barn in a location where your child will have independent access to the toys stored in the pockets. Now use this activity as a way of teaching that belongings should be put away in their own special places after play. Your child will already be used to seeing the toys in their "places." Talk with your child about where each toy belongs, in which pocket. Then take away one toy and ask your child to put it back in the right place. Next take away two toys and have your child put each one back in the right place. Then go up to three, and so on. The idea, through play and practice, is to help your child learn to put all of them away in their designated spots in the Toy Barn, which will give him a sense of accomplishment and independence.

Toy Bag

Age Range: Birth to Three Years

Objective: To have an easy way to transport toys from one place to another. With this easy-to-use bag, you will have an easy way to put out and clean up a group of your child's toys.

Description: A laundry bag, tote bag, or beach bag used to hold toys.

Materials:

• A cloth bag of your choice

Directions: Select a bag of your choice. Fill it with a collection of your child's toys.

How to Use and Enjoy This Toy

Having one or more bags of toys will give you an easy way to take toys with you and set them up wherever you go, to a different room, to someone else's house, or to somewhere else where you will have to keep your child busy. Having groups of toys set up in this way will make it easy for you to transport toys at a moment's notice.

8

Toys About Colors

Color Recognition

As soon as your baby can see, he begins to recognize colors. The toys described in this chapter—Color Boxes, Color Books, Color Cards, Color Crates, and their variations—will give your baby experience in discriminating among colors. These toys will also teach your baby the names of the colors over time and help him develop manipulative skills as he plays with the objects. Besides encouraging play, creativity, and fun, these color toys also teach important basic concepts. Through handling items in the Color Boxes, your child will have the opportunity to experience many concepts—hard and soft, rough and smooth, big and little, and many more. He will also have the opportunity to learn many different vocabulary words as each of the different items are referred to during the course of the play. Color Books will be filled with interesting pictures that will delight as well as inform your child.

Color Boxes

FIGURE 8.1   Color Boxes

Age Range: Birth to Three Years

Objective: To teach your baby to identify colors and to provide experience in manipulating objects and developing academic concepts such as sorting, sequencing, vocabulary development, and counting.

Description: Four large, lidded containers with red, yellow, blue, or green tops, each containing colored objects corresponding to the color on the container's lid.

Materials:

- Four large plastic containers with lids; quart, half-gallon, or gallon size work well
- Four colored sheets; one piece each of red, yellow, blue, and green, large enough to cover the container lids—texture of your choice, such as felt, smooth contact paper, or construction paper
- Scissors
- White glue (or paste, if using construction paper)

- Small objects to fit inside the containers; three or four in each of the colors—red, yellow, blue, and green

Directions: Match one colored sheet to each container so that each container is represented by a different color. Trace the container lid on the sheet you've chosen, cut out the tracing, and paste the red, yellow, blue, or green circle on the matching lid, using a different color for each container. Using textured materials for these lids, such as soft felt or smooth contact paper, adds an extra dimension to the toy, giving baby something interesting to feel as well as to look at. Glue or paste the tracing to the lid of the corresponding container.

Fill each container with objects of the same (or nearly the same) color. For example, red objects you collected belong in the container with the red lid. Do the same for the other Color Boxes. Be sure the objects you choose are clean and safe for very young children to play with—not too small to be swallowed, too rough, broken, or with sharp edges. In addition, choose objects for the Color Boxes that are interesting for your child to look at and touch. Short red ribbons, green plastic blocks, yellow colored nets from bags of lemons (with the lead staple cut off), blue plastic coffee scoops, scraps of colored paper, and odd pieces from old toys make intriguing box fillers. Scour your house for items you are not using and otherwise might throw away. Every household contains hidden treasures like these!

How to Use and Enjoy This Toy

Birth to Eighteen Months.　Babies and toddlers love to empty and fill containers, and they are attracted to items with texture. Play with one container at a time. Watch your child empty the toys one by one and then put them back, or make up another game that fits your child's level of interest. One idea is to turn the container upside down and hide one of the objects under it.

Another idea is to count the items one by one. As you or your child handles each item, call it by its color, "red ribbon, red spool, red block," and so on. Grandma and Grandpa will make up their own games with these boxes, and everyone who participates with baby will refer to the containers by their color. Before long, your child will be able to bring you exactly the Color Box you ask for, and one day you will hear your child name the color for himself. Your baby is never too young to play with this toy. Even if he does not sit up yet, you can hold him on your lap and name the brightly colored items as you show them.

Eighteen Months to Three Years.   More advanced color activities are appropriate now.

Stacking game. Stacking the Color Boxes is fun! Quart-size containers are best for stacking, but containers of other sizes can be stacked as well. You and your child might want to use two, three, or all four of the Color Boxes for play.

Sorting game. To begin with, open two of the Color Boxes and dump their contents on the floor. Mix them up and then help your child sort the items by color so that they can be returned to the appropriate Color Box. Or sort the items by size, shape, or texture.

Treasure hunt. You and your child can play creatively with the Color Box items in any way you choose. Use as many vocabulary words as possible as you talk about and play with each item. A silk flower can be described as "red," "small," "soft," "fragrant (if it is)," "a rose," "pretty," and more. Your toddler or two-year-old can carry a Color Box and collect his own objects for it from around the house or yard (supervised, of course). Or place color objects all around a room and send him on a treasure hunt to find the right items for a certain Color Box. He can enjoy filling up two or more Color Boxes, depending on how elaborate you wish to make the game. Or give your child a beach pail. Let him collect items in it that are the same color as the pail.

Color Books

FIGURE 8.2   **Color Books**

FIGURE 8.3   **Color Books**

Age Range: Birth to Three Years

Objective: To teach your baby to identify colors. Color Books also provide an opportunity to learn words.

Description: Four books, each a different color, made from four three-ring folders in different colors, filled with colored construction paper that matches the color of the folder. (You may use white paper for this instead.) Each Color Book contains cut out pictures from magazines or catalogs and textured items in the same color as the folder. One picture belongs on each page, with a simple label beneath the picture written in a black or color marker.

Materials:

- Four three-ring folders, one each in red, yellow, blue, and green
- Colored construction paper; five sheets each of red, yellow, blue, and green *or* twenty sheets (five for each book) of white paper
- Three-hole punch
- Assortment of old magazines, catalogs, or other sources of brightly colored pictures
- Textured items, such as a six-inch ribbon, a six-by-six-inch piece of netting, and a six-by-six-inch piece of felt
- Scissors
- White glue, paste, or double-stick tape
- Markers or crayons in red, yellow, blue, and green; or black
- Clear contact paper, optional

Directions: Using the three-hole punch, punch holes in the construction paper so that it will fit into the folders. Place five sheets in a matching color, or five white sheets, in each of the folders. Using the marker or crayon in the matching color or black, write the name of the book on each folder as appropriate: "Red Book," "Yellow Book," "Blue Book," or "Green Book." Cut out colored pictures from magazines or catalogs and paste them, one per page, in the appropriate Color Book.

Write simple labels for each picture, using a black marker or crayon in books with colored pages. For books made with white-paper pages, use a marker in the featured color.

For children between birth and eighteen months, use two-word phrases for the label, such as, "Blue ball," "Red car," and "Yellow ribbon." For children age eighteen months to three years, labels can be longer; for example, "My blue ball," "The red car," "The ribbon is yellow." Ribbons, nets, or other textured materials are also excellent for these books, especially if the folders you collect have pockets in which to store them.

Laminate or cover the pages with clear contact paper to make them more durable, if you like. You do not have to fill all five pages of the book at once—make up a page or two at a time, and add other items to your book as you find them.

How to Use and Enjoy This Toy

Birth to Eighteen Months. Read these books to your baby or toddler. Point to each word as you read it. After many repetitions and when your child is ready, let him participate by saying any of the words he recognizes. In time, ask your toddler to bring you a particular Color Book to read, and let him choose the correct book.

Eighteen Months to Three Years. Continue to read these books with your child as he grows, pointing out each word. At this stage, let your child be the primary reader. Fill in by saying the words he has trouble recognizing as you point to them.

Also, let your child participate with you as much as possible in choosing the pictures for these books.

Color Cards

FIGURE 8.4   Color Cards

Age Range: Birth to Three Years

Objective: To teach your child to recognize four words describing color—"red," "yellow," "blue," and "green"—by repetition and familiarity.

Description: Eight double-sided five-by-eight-inch index cards with the "color word" written in color on one side and in black on the other side. Use the eight cards to mix and match for many activities.

Materials:

- Sixteen five-by-eight-inch index cards
- Clear contact paper or laminating material (enough to cover the whole card with about a half-inch border all around it
- Scissors
- White glue, paste, or double-stick tape
- Markers or crayons in red, yellow, blue, green, and black

Directions: Write "Red" with a red marker or crayon on two index cards. Start each word with a capital letter and use lowercase letters for the rest. Make borders in matching colors around the edges of the cards to make them more interesting. Make two cards in the same manner for each of the remaining colors: yellow, blue, and green. Next, make a set of eight matching Color Cards with the words and borders written in black. Make the letters large and clear.

Glue or paste the cards with the black writing on the backs of the matching cards with the colored writing, so that the color named is written in color on one side and in black on the other. Cover each card with clear contact paper or laminate each one, for a total of eight versatile cards, two representing each color.

How to Use and Enjoy This Toy

Birth to Twelve Months.   During this year, let your baby direct your play. Start by showing your baby the Red Card on the red side only. Let him get used to the word. Then show him the back of the card with the word "Red" written in black. Babies like to hold and play with cards, so let your baby handle the card when he is ready. There are no rules; whichever side faces up next time, name the color as written.

Once you sense baby's familiarity with this card, introduce the second Red Card. However your child looks at or matches the two cards is fine. Your role is to keep naming them as "red" when you see them. Once you feel that your baby is ready for a change, follow the same procedure for yellow and the other Color Cards. Use the card pairs only; at this point, do not mix the different color cards.

Twelve to Twenty-four Months.   Once your toddler has familiarity with each of the four color words—red, yellow, green, and blue—give him *all* the cards to play with. Now you are ready to make up your own games with the cards: Match them to colored objects in the room, hide them, count them, and more. Keep naming the words as the cards are used. Enjoy!

Two to Three Years.   Now that you are past free-form play with the cards, introduce a matching game. Feel free to make up your own variations.

   Match game 1. For example, you could put all the cards in a pile. See how many matched pairs you and your child can each get until the cards are all drawn from the pile. Put all the cards back and start again.

   Match game 2. Select four cards in four different colors. Take turns picking cards from the pile and matching them to one of the four original colors. Next, match black to color, and then black to black.

Color Crates

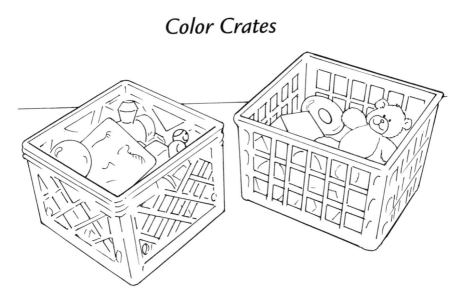

FIGURE 8.5   Color Crates

Age Range: Birth to Three Years

Objective: To increase color awareness; to use that awareness to create an effective system for rotating toys.

Description: Four colored crates in red, yellow, blue, and green. Toys of the appropriate color are stored in each of the crates.

Materials:

- Four colored crates in red, yellow, blue, and green
- Colored toys or household play materials that match the colors. The number of toys in each crate will vary depending on the size of the toys you have available in each color.

Directions: Collect your child's toys or other safe household play materials and sort them by color into the four colored crates. Stack the crates on top of each other or side by side, whichever way fits your available space better.

How to Use and Enjoy This Toy

Birth to Eighteen Months.   Bring out one of the four toy crates for short play periods, such as one day, several days, or one week. Keep the toy box out as long as the toys in it hold your child's interest. When your child begins to lose interest, put the crate back in the stack and offer another crate in a different color. Use all four Color Crates in rotation. Mention to your child the color of each crate you bring out. That is one way to enhance the color-learning process.

Eighteen Months to Three Years.   Bring out a number of toys from each of the four Color Crates and let your child sort the toys into the appropriate colored crates. Help as much or as little as is necessary.

For play, use only one toy crate at a time at first. Let your child select the crate for his play. Teach your child to return all the toys to the crate when he is finished playing with them, pointing out that they belong together in the crate because they are all the same color. Let him select another crate for play as soon as the other toys have been put away.

When your child is ready, let him choose *two* crates for play. Cleanup will become a little more advanced. If he is ready for this activity, he will enjoy the process of sorting the toys before returning the Color Crates to their proper storage location.

9

Toys About Letters

Letter Recognition

Until recently, researchers considered learning the letters of the alphabet to be an abstract task for children. But in fact, children learn their letters in much the same way that they learn to recognize and name other pictures that they see often. We live in a world of signs and writing, and these common symbols exert a major environmental influence. It isn't too early to introduce your child to his letters as a baby.

Letter Cards

FIGURE 9.1   Letter Cards

Age Range: Birth to Three Years

Objective: To teach your child to recognize and name the letters of the alphabet by repetition and familiarity.

Description: Thirteen four-by-six-inch cards, each with a different letter of the alphabet on either side of the card. A looped string is attached to a corner of each card, so that it can hang from a highchair or doorknob. If the highchair has no post from which to hang the card, the letter card may be hung from a cabinet handle near the highchair. If you don't find natural spots for hanging these letter-card toys in your house, create a place for these letters by attaching several stick-on hooks to a convenient wall, such as a kitchen wall near baby's highchair.

Materials:

- Thirteen four-by-six-inch index cards
- One package of stick-on capital letters, two to three inches high (available in office supply stores)
- Hole punch
- Thirteen pieces of string, yarn, or ribbon, each about twelve inches long
- Scissors
- Clear contact paper or laminating material

Directions: Affix letters to index cards, back to back starting with "A" backed by "B," and continuing to "Y" backed by "Z." Cover each card with clear contact paper or laminate it.

Punch a hole in a top corner of each card. Insert one piece of string, yarn, or ribbon through the hole in each card. Tie the ends of the string together to form a loop.

How to Use and Enjoy This Toy

Birth to One Year.   Start with the A/B card. Let your baby play with it. He will probably like having a card with a "loop handle" on it to hold and manipulate. When you see him looking at the "B," say, "Oh, you are looking at the 'B!' You can point out the "A" as well, but both of you will have lots more fun with the "B," one of the first sounds a baby learns to make. Name the "B" in the same way that you would casually name other items in your baby's environment, such as food being eaten, a cup, a spoon, and so on. Introduce this letter card just as casually.

When you realize that your baby recognizes "B," put "B" away and take out the C/D card. Again, let your baby play with it. When you see him looking at the "D," say, "Oh, you are looking at the 'D!'" You can point out the "C" as well, but both of you will have more fun with "D," which is considered the second sound a baby learns to make.

Introduce this letter card just as casually as you did with "B." Just as with "B," you will realize your baby recognizes the "D."

After "B" and "D," consider introducing your child to the first letter of his name. Continue introducing to your baby Letter Cards, one by one, until your baby recognizes all the letters. Go back to "A" and introduce it. Continue with the rest in alphabetical order if you like.

Remember, Letter Cards are your baby's toys, things for fun. They are available for your baby just like any other pictures—of clowns, ducks, bunnies, or anything else—that you choose to show your baby. These are pictures to look at, enjoy, and remember.

With Letter Cards, you will not be your baby's only teacher. Others who see your baby looking at a letter will probably affirm what it is for baby: "Oh, you're holding a 'B.'" Such playful repetition enhances learning in a very positive way.

One to Two Years.   Now that your toddler is moving around more and enjoying more fine-motor control, he can do more with these cards. He can put them on and take them off doorknobs, the highchair, cabinet handles, and any other hooks that you have created for him to find. Your toddler only needs to see the letters over and over and hear you name them from time to time for them to become a permanent part of his learning.

Two to Three Years.   Familiar with all the letters, your two-year-old will probably enjoy games with the letters that connect them with letter sounds: Have fun matching the letters to beginning sounds of specific objects. Take turns picking one of the thirteen letters. Then take turns bringing the letter on one of your cards to an object that starts with that letter. For example, you can place "D" on a doorknob. "B" can go on a book. Place "T" on a towel, and "K" on a key. Have fun with the letters, moving them from place to place all around the house. Help your child as little or as much as is necessary with this matching activity.

Beginning spelling. It's easy to create simple spelling activities with these cards. It's best to start by spelling your child's name. His name is, and will always be, his favorite word. Take advantage of that interest to develop many teaching opportunities from that single word.

Note: To spell your child's name and other words using the letter cards may require a letter that is on the back of a card already used, or may require two or three examples of the same letter. You may have to make extra cards for this activity.

The name game. After making the extra cards, if needed, spell your child's name. Take away one of the letters and ask your child to put it back in the right place. Next, ask your child to remove one letter so that you can put it back in the right place.

The rest of this name activity is in your hands. Let your child take the lead. Create games with these letters at whatever learning level is appropriate for your child. The game might be to take away and replace two letters from the child's name; it might be to mix up all the letters and then reorder them; it might be to find or make up a smaller word contained in his name. This activity now belongs to you and your child. Create and enjoy!

Other high-interest words. When you have finished your name fun, go on to spelling and playing with other short words. Popular suggestions are your name, "Mom," "Dad, "Mommy," "Daddy," other family member names, pet names, "Cat," "Dog," and any particular favorite words that your child may say often.

Pick-a-letter game. Return to the letter cards and make words by picking out letters from the whole alphabet. You might want to pick letters and then find words or titles from magazines and newspapers that contain those letters. A reminder: These are letter cards for fun, and you and your child will probably think of many interesting uses for them. Play with them and have fun with them; don't use them to drill your child about the alphabet.

Letter Toy Boxes

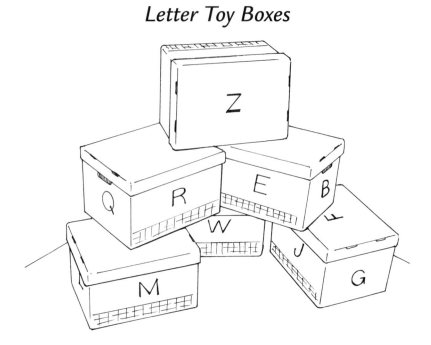

FIGURE 9.2   Letter Toy Boxes

Age Range: Birth to Three Years

Objective: To give your child in a play setting familiarity with the letters of the alphabet and to give you a system for rotating toys.

Description: Six cardboard filing boxes, each with large capital letters written on the lid and sides of the box, one letter per surface. Six boxes provide exposure for the twenty-six letters of the alphabet.

Materials:

- Six office filing boxes with lids
- Markers

Directions: Choose a marker. Print a large, clear capital A in the middle of the lid of the first box. Next, print the letters B,

C, D, and E on each of the box's four sides, one letter per side, centering each letter.

Using the same or a different marker, print a large, clear capital F on the lid of the second box. Print the next four letters of the alphabet on each of the second box's four sides in the same way as before. Choose the same or a different marker and a third box. On the lid print a large, clear capital K as before. Print four more letters on each of the third box's four sides, one letter per side, centering each letter.

Proceed with the fourth box in a similar fashion, using a P for the lid. For the fifth box, write a U on the lid and the next four letters of the alphabet on each of the four sides.

Write a Z on the lid of the sixth box. For this box, keep the sides empty, place some other interesting pictures on them, *or* leave them blank as scribble or drawing areas for your child. These are your toys. Make them as simple or as decorative as you wish.

How to Use and Enjoy This Toy

You cannot go wrong with boxes as playthings! Babies, toddlers, and two-year-olds love them. Like the Color Crates (see page 111), these boxes can be used as an effective toy storage system. Letter Boxes are different because they contain toys of any color. Letter Boxes give you the advantage of the visual alphabetical order to help you rotate the toys for your child. If you take out one box a day or every few days or one a week, the six boxes will space the toys available to your child nicely. Keeping the boxes in view—perhaps in your child's room—means that your child will see the letters often, which will help him become familiar with them.

Facilitate learning these letters by making frequent remarks about them, such as, "You opened the lid with the 'E' on it," or "Look what I see, a 'B' just like the one hanging on your doorknob." Your child will have the opportunity to enjoy the many toys inside these boxes, and you will have the additional opportunity to point out and teach the letters on the outside.

Do not forget that the toy box is a toy, all by itself. It comes complete with a lid ready for play. Once he has finished playing with the toys inside, do not be surprised if you find your little one hard at play with the box.

Alphabet Boxes

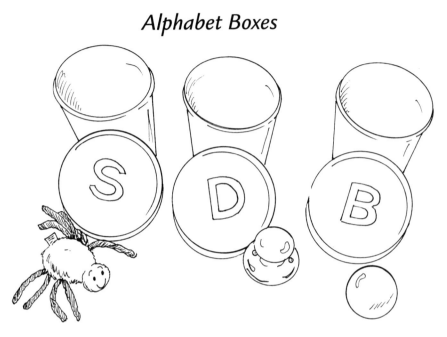

FIGURE 9.3   Alphabet Boxes

Age Range: Birth to Three Years

Objective: To teach letter recognition and letter sounds.

Description: Any number of plastic containers up to twenty-six, each showing a different letter of the alphabet on the lid and small, safe, interesting objects inside that start with the sound of the letter on the top.

Materials:

- Plastic containers with lids, any number up to twenty-six
- Stick-on capital letters—two, three, four, or five inches in size (available in most office supply stores)
- Small, safe, interesting objects to fit in the containers

Directions: Select a container with a lid, such as a margarine tub, from your recycle bin. Place a stick-on letter on the top. (A good first choice is a "B," because that is one of the first sounds baby makes.) Find small, safe, interesting objects that start with that letter and place them inside the container, such as a ball or a little brush. Stick a "D" on the next container and fill it with items or toys that start with "D," such as a small plush dog or a doll. For a third container, choose the first letter of your child's name. After that, make as many containers as you would like, up to twenty-six for all the letters in the alphabet.

How to Use and Enjoy This Toy

Birth to Eighteen Months.   Use this toy largely as you used the Color Boxes in Chapter 8 (see page 103). Babies and toddlers love to empty and fill containers, and they also love to handle textured items.

Empty-and-fill game. Choose one container at a time. Watch your child empty the toys one by one and then put them back, or make up another game that fits your child's interest level. As you or your child handle each item, name it and then refer to the letter. For example, if using the B box you might say, "Ball. Ball starts with 'B,'" and point to the B. "Bag. Bag starts with 'B,'" and point to the letter again. "Box. Box starts with 'B,'" and point again. Grandma and Grandpa will make up their own games with these boxes, and everyone who visits will have their own ideas too. Before long, your child will be able to bring you the Letter Box you ask for, and one day you will hear your child say the letter spontaneously.

Eighteen Months to Three Years.   More advanced letter activities are appropriate now. Quart-size containers are probably the best for stacking, but the others will stack as well.

Sorting game. You and your child might want to use two, three, or four Letter Boxes for play at this time. I suggest that you start by opening two containers, mixing up their contents on the floor, and then sorting them back into the appropriate boxes.

Describing games. You and your child can play creatively with the items in the boxes in any way you like. Be sure to use as many different describing words as possible as you talk about and play with each item. It isn't necessary to limit your descriptions to words that match the correct letter sound, but if you decide to play this way, you might find it to be challenging and fun. Examples are a "blue ball," a "big blue ball," a "darling dog," or a "doll's dress."

Scavenger hunt-and-sort. You and others will probably have a lot of fun playing with your child and making up different games using the Letter Boxes and their contents. Now that your toddler or two-year-old can walk, he might be able to carry a basket or other container and collect objects from around the house by himself. Together you can decide in which Letter Box to put the items, according to their names.

Hide-and-seek game. You can also place letter objects around a room and have him go on a hunt to find the items. If two or more letters are part of the game, you and he can enjoy sorting his finds into their proper Letter Boxes.

Letter Notebook

FIGURE 9.4   Letter Notebook

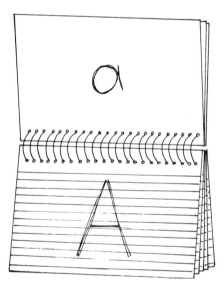

FIGURE 9.5   Letter Notebook

Age Range: Birth to Three Years

Objective: To give your child another opportunity to become familiar with the letters.

Description: A four-by-six-inch spiral-bound, index-card notebook containing the letters of the alphabet in capital let-

ters, one per page, and the lowercase letters on the flip sides of
the pages.

Materials:

- One four-by-six-inch spiral-bound, index-card notebook
- Crayons

Directions: On each front-side page print a different letter of the
alphabet in order from A to Z. On each back-side page print the
corresponding lowercase letter. If you use a different color for each
of the capital letters, make the matching lowercase letter in the
matching color. Print the letters as big and as clearly as possible.

How to Use and Enjoy This Toy

One to Two Years.   This is your toddler's book to enjoy holding
(and shortly, turning the pages of). Index-card pages are quite
durable and provide an appropriate fine-motor activity for your
child. Whatever page is open for play will feature a letter. Your
child will like looking at the letters. Help your child to open
the book from front to back and to notice the capital letters.
When convenient, casually name them in phrases such as, "Oh,
you found the 'B,' or "I see a 'W.'"

Two to Three Years.   Now your two-year-old can enjoy this book
on a much higher level. Let him take the lead. If he wants to
name the letters he sees, that's fine. If he asks you to name them,
that is fine too. If he shows you a capital letter that he knows,
such as an "A," you can turn the page over and say something
like, "That's an 'A' too." If he shows you a lowercase letter, say
something like, "b." Then turn the page and say something like,
"Here's a 'B' too." As with the other toys in this book, use this
toy in different ways. Let your child be the guide, and the two of
you will probably figure out many different learning activities.

Letter Pillows

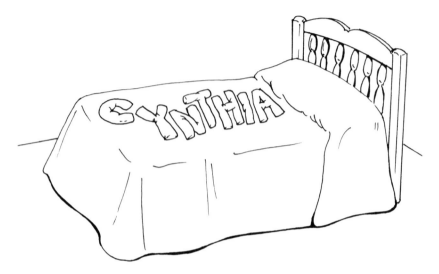

FIGURE 9.6   Letter Pillows

Age Range: Birth to Three Years

Objective: To use letters to introduce your child to the spelling of his name.

Description: Letter pillows placed in order to spell out your child's name.

Materials:

- Two sixteen-by-fourteen-inch pieces of material for each pillow letter
- Patterns to make the pillows, one per letter
- Needle and thread
- Thimble
- Fabric scissors
- Fabric pencil, regular pencil, or pen
- Pillow stuffing

- Sewing machine (optional)
- Readymade pillows (optional)

Directions: You have options for completing this project. Choose the option that is most comfortable for you. Here are some possibilities.

Option 1. Choose fabric that does not unravel when it is cut. Cut out two rectangles, sixteen by fourteen inches, for each pillow. On them, draw with a fabric pencil, regular pencil, or pen the shape of the letter that you want to cut out. Cut out your letter in duplicate, using this pattern. Put the two pieces of fabric together face to face, and sew together along the edges, leaving an opening at one spot for pillow stuffing. Turn the pillow right-side-out for stuffing. Stuff the pillow and then sew up the open spot. Repeat this process to make letter pillows for all the letters in your child's name.

Option 2. Buy patterns for the letters of your child's name at a fabric store. Purchase all the supplies you need to follow the pattern and make the pillows, as the pattern directs.

Option 3. Ask at the fabric store if they will make up letter pillows to order.

Option 4. Buy readymade pillows that spell out your child's name from a baby store or other store where such novelty items are sold.

How to Use and Enjoy This Toy

Birth to Eighteen Months.   Just as you expose your child to the names of his stuffed animals, so you can introduce him to the "names" of his stuffed pillows, such as "J," "E," and "D." Don't leave the pillows in baby's crib; keep them out of baby's reach and entertain him with the colorful pillows as you would show him a rattle or other toy.

Eighteen Months to Three Years.   Once baby is old enough, you might want to put these pillows out as decorations on your child's bed. First show your child how to place them in the proper order to spell his name. In time he can help you place them in order. After that, he will be able to put all of them out himself. Yes, you're right: Your child will be spelling his name!

Magnetic Letters

FIGURE 9.7   Magnetic Letters

Age Range: Eighteen Months to Three Years
Objective: To gain experience with letters in a hands-on way.
Description: Two sets of magnetic letters, capital and lowercase, and a magnetic board.
Materials:

- Two sets of magnetic letters, capital and lowercase
- Magnetic board

Directions: Place the letters on this board in the most appropriate way for your child. Use either all capitals, capitals with lowercase, or make words.

How to Use and Enjoy This Toy

Start with capital letters only. Start by offering your child the capital letters only. Let him manipulate and enjoy these colorful letters. As with the other letter activities, comment in a casual way on the letters he picks up.

Add lowercase letters to the play area. When you notice that your child recognizes some lowercase letters, add them to his play area.

Making words. When he is ready for words, display those as well. Be free and open with this activity. As always, let your child be the guide during playtime. Have fun naming letters and words in ways that you think will help your child learn.

Alphabet Blocks

FIGURE 9.8   Alphabet Blocks

Age Range: Birth to Three Years
Objective: To teach recognition of the alphabet letters.
Description: Store-bought alphabet blocks.
Materials:

- One set of store-bought alphabet blocks, three inches square is the preferred size

Directions: Alphabet blocks that are three inches square are preferred, but can be hard to find. Use two-inch-square blocks if those are available; other block sizes can be used as well if necessary.

How to Use and Enjoy This Toy

Birth to One Year.   Alphabet blocks used to be the standard way that children learned their letters. During your baby's first year, he will enjoy playing with just one block at a time. When you see your baby looking at any one letter, name the letter for him.

One to Two Years.   During this year your toddler will begin stacking blocks. He will start with two and may progress to one or two more. Continue to name the letters for baby on the blocks that he has chosen for play.

Two to Three Years.   Now block building expands to about eight blocks. You and your two-year-old can participate in simple building activities. At this stage, say things like, "Here is the 'B,'" and "Pass me the top block with the 'D' on it." Play in your own creative way as you would with any blocks or stacking materials and enjoy the added opportunity to expose your child to letters with these alphabet blocks.

10

Toys About Numbers

Number Concepts

Very young children can learn numerals as symbols just as easily as they can learn letters as symbols. Numerals are learned as symbols before the numerical concepts behind the symbols are internalized. Although in the beginning the idea is to foster a child's recognition of numerals, the numerical concept will soon follow. Both concepts are introduced and reinforced by activities emphasizing repetition and familiarity.

Number Books

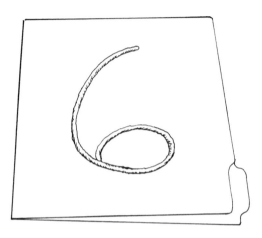

FIGURE 10.1   Number Books

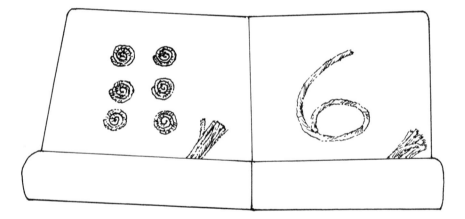

FIGURE 10.2   Number Books

Age Range: Birth to Three Years

Objective: To teach recognition of the numerals from 0 to 10 and to introduce the number concepts by repetition and familiarity.

Description: Eleven books made out of file folders, each about a single number beginning with 0 and continuing to 10 ("1 Book," "2 Book," "3 Book," and so on). Each book has the number on the front cover, a corresponding number of dots on the next page, a number on the next page, and the corresponding number of dots on the last page. All the number books are made in the same way.

Materials:

- Eleven nine-by-twelve-inch file folders, various colors
- One package thick yarn, the type used in children's hair or for gift wrap
- Scissors
- White glue

Directions: For each folder, open to lay flat. Fold up the open folder from the bottom to make a section about three inches deep along the bottom of the inside of the folder. Start with the "1 Book" and then make them in order up to the "10 Book." Make "0" the last book. For the "1 Book," take the yarn and cut it to make two "1's" and two dots. Glue one "1" on the cover, one dot on the left-hand side of the open folder, the other "1" on the right-hand side of the open folder, and one dot on the back of the folder. For the "2 Book," follow the same procedures. Go on to complete eleven Number Books. As you do each book, use the same color yarn throughout the book. For the dot configurations in each book, use playing card configurations.

For the folded-up sections of each book, place yarn pieces for counting that match the number. For example, for the "1 Book," place one piece of yarn in each pocket. For the "2 Book," place two pieces of yarn in each pocket. Cut the pieces of yarn for the pockets about three inches in length. That is a good length for easy manipulation.

How to Use and Enjoy Your New Toy

Birth to Eighteen Months.   Start with the "1 Book" and use it as you would any other book with your baby. When you read it, point to each piece of yarn, rub your baby's fingers or hand over it and say, "one." Whether you are going over the numeral or the dot, you call it the same thing, "one." Your baby will probably like this experience a lot. The texture and the color should be pleasing. After you finish reading the book, you can take out the yarn piece in the left-hand folder and say, "one." Put that one back and take out the yarn piece in the right-hand folder. Then count that one.

When you feel your baby has a good grasp of the number "1" by showing you some kind of recognition, go on to the "2 Book." Use that one in a similar fashion to the way you used the "1 Book." When you feel your baby knows that one well, go on to the "3 Book." Continue slowly and thoroughly with these books up to the number "10" and then add the "0." Show your baby all the books that have been mastered from time to time during the whole process. This will help your baby to keep a solid grasp of all the numbers he has previously learned.

Eighteen Months to Three Years.   Have lots of fun with these books. Let your child be the guide. If he knows the numbers, enjoy them together as he reads the books to you. If he does not know the numbers, introduce them just as you would have in the birth-to-eighteen-months stage. Make up all kinds of games. Always participate in the activity. Take your turn as you put the books in order, match yarn pieces from the left and right pockets in each folder, and go around your house counting all kinds of objects like crayons, pencils, cotton balls, and other interesting household items.

Sort o' Cards

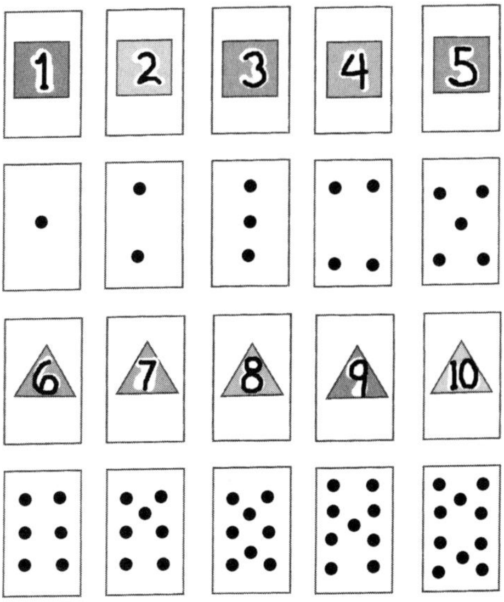

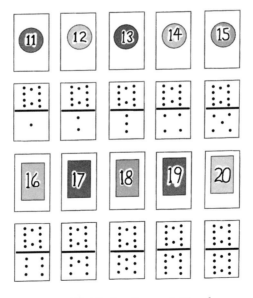

FIGURE 10.3 Sort o' Cards

FIGURE 10.4 Sort o' Cards

Age Range: Birth to Three Years

Objective: To provide your child with clear visual representations of numerals and beginning number concepts.

Description: Two sets of matching cards made from three-by-five-inch index cards numbered from 1 to 20. On the back of each card are the appropriate numbers of dots to match the numeral. For numbers over 10, the dots are arranged to develop an understanding of groups of ten. One set is numbered in black with orange dots. The other is numbered in orange with black dots. Cards 1 through 5 have squares on the front, 6 through 10 have triangles, 11 through 15 have circles, and 16 through 20 have rectangles. Each of the shapes is colored in one of the four main colors—red, yellow, blue, and green.

Materials:

- Forty three-by-five-inch index cards
- Six crayons: red, yellow, blue, green, black, and orange, or markers in those colors
- Stick-on dots (optional)
- Ruler
- Clear contact paper or laminating material

Directions: Begin by making one set of twenty cards. Then make the second set. Number twenty cards in black from 1 to 20. On the back of each card make a corresponding number of orange dots. Use the standard dot configuration from a deck of cards. For numbers 11 through 20, use the standard configuration for ten. Then draw a line under the group of ten dots. Under this line add the correct number of additional dots. This means the card for 11 has a group of ten dots above the line and the eleventh dot below the line. You can use crayons to make the numbers and dots, or you can use stick-on numbers and dots, which are available in most office supply stores.

For cards 1 through 5, surround the numerals by squares. On card number 1, make the square red; on 2, make the square yellow; 3, blue; 4, green; 5, red. For cards 6 through 10, surround the numerals by triangles. Make 6 yellow; 7 blue; 8 green; 9 red; 10 yellow. For cards 11 through 15, surround the numerals by circles. Make 11 blue; 12 green; 13 red; 14 yellow; 15 blue. For cards 16 through 20, surround the numerals by rectangles. Make 16 green; 17 red; 18 yellow; 19 blue; 20 green.

Number the second set of cards with an orange marker. On the back make black dots to match. This color scheme is exactly opposite from the first set. It will facilitate separating the cards into two sets and make clearer the matching activities of numerals to dots and dots to numerals.

Because there is a large number of cards to make, it will be more fun to make a few cards at a time. If you start with cards 1 through 5 from both sets, you will already have a set of cards that you can begin using. Then you can make a few more at a time and add them to your set gradually. This game activity can be created over time and then grow as your child grows.

How to Use and Enjoy This Toy

Birth to One Year.   Cards 1 through 5 from each set can be used as baby toys. You can cover them with clear contact paper or laminate them. Since babies love cards and paper, cards with large, clear numbers on them will be appealing. While your baby does all the playing, you sit back and name the cards. In the beginning, give him only cards 1 and 2 from each set. Whichever side is up, the dot or the numeral, call it by the number. In time, introduce the other three cards.

One to Two Years.   When your toddler is ready, use cards 1 through 5 from both sets for matching activities: numerals to numerals, dots to numerals, and dots to dots. You can put the five black numeral cards out. Then you can give him the orange numeral cards, one at a time, to match. He can do it first with the orange numeral side, then with the black dot side, and then with the black dot side again, but this time with the original five cards turned to the orange dot side.

There is another game you can play with your toddler with these cards. Using only cards 1 through 5, one at a time, show him the numeral side. Then show the dot side so that he associates the two. Then start with the dot side and ask him to try to say the numeral before you show it to him on the other side. The first few times you will probably show the numeral first, but after a while he will be saying the numeral before you turn the card to show it.

Two to Three Years.   When your two-year-old is ready, continue the toddler activities with the higher numbers. Introduce one number at a time from each set, as you would bring out any new toy. For example, if your child is matching well "1" to one dot, "2" to two dots, "3" to three dots, "4" to four dots, and "5" to five dots, mix into his cards for this activity the two "6" cards. Be sure not to place demands on yourself or your child to rush through learning a set of numbers. Remember, these are toys to be played with, to be learned by repetition and familiarity.

Sorting activities are also fun for two-year-olds, and you can use any of the cards for these. Decide whether you would like to sort by color or shape. Set up where the piles will be. If by color, show your child which is for red, yellow, blue, and green. If by shape, show him which is for circles, squares, triangles, and rectangles. Playing along and taking your turn can make the activity more enjoyable for you and your preschooler.

Counting Objects

FIGURE 10.5   Counting Objects

Age Range: Birth to Three Years

Objective: To teach number concepts and counting.

Description: Objects in the household that are in specified groupings.

Materials: Objects in the household that are in specified groupings

Directions: Find objects in your house that are already in specified number groupings.

How to Use and Enjoy This Toy

Birth to One Year.   Take your baby with you on a trip around the house looking at all kinds of interesting things in it. If you find something like one vase, you can say to your baby, "one vase." You could also add, "one flower." Maybe you have a grouping of two candles, three books, or four pictures. You could also point them out as such. A stop at a mirror is recommended too. You will easily see two eyes, two ears, one nose, and one mouth. Moreover, knowing that his ten fingers and ten toes will be with you wherever you go, you will never run out of something to count.

One to Two Years.   Take your toddler by the hand this time and allow him to lead you around the house. As he spontaneously points out different objects, label them as "one table," "two chairs," "three towels," and more.

Two to Three Years.   Add counting to as many activities as possible. If you are folding clothes, count the socks, towels, shirts, and more. When outside, count trees and other objects. When in a restaurant, count the sugars. Take your child up and down steps, if you can find some. Chant, "one, two, three, look at me" as he goes up and "three, two, one, that was fun" as he goes down. Create your own counting fun.

Dice

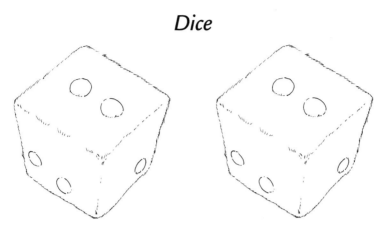

FIGURE 10.6   Dice

Age Range: One to Three Years
Objective: To teach number configurations and number concepts.
Description: Large soft dice.
Materials: Large soft dice
Directions: Purchase store-bought soft dice.

How to Use and Enjoy This Toy

One to Two Years.   Each of you take one of the dice. Take turns throwing your die with your toddler. Whatever it lands on, you name the number. For example, if he throws two dots, you say something like, "You got two." When you throw your die, you can call out your number. In time, he can be the one to say both what he gets and what you get. The game is nice because each throw provides a surprise.

Two to three Years.   Just as before, each of you take one of the dice. This time, however, you both throw them together. When they land, you count the dots added together. Let your two-year-old participate as much as possible in the counting.

Sponge Numbers

FIGURE 10.7   Sponge Numbers

Age Range: Birth to Three Years

Objective: To teach number recognition.

Description: Set of numbers made from soft sponges. Have at least one number each beginning with 1 and going up to 10.

Materials:

- Twelve soft sponges
- Pencil
- Scissors
- Set of store-bought number sponges (optional)

Directions: Draw with a pencil the outline of the number you are going to cut out from the sponge. Then cut out the number. Start with the number "1." Then continue in order up to "10." Then make the "0."

How to Use and Enjoy This Toy

Birth to Eighteen Months.   Use a Number Sponge one at a time. Your baby will enjoy the color and the texture of the number. Whenever you hand one to your baby, be sure to say what number it is. These are a natural for play at bathtime.

Eighteen Months to Three Years.   Play is the essence of this activity. The colors and texture of these Number Sponges will immediately invite play. As you and your child play, name the numbers in a natural way. Continue to use in the bath.

Domino Number Cards

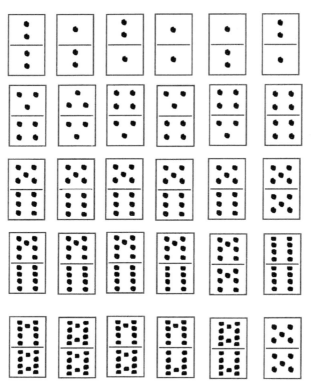

FIGURE 10.8   Domino Number Cards

Age Range: Two to Three Years

Objective: To teach number configurations and number concepts.

Description: Five sets of Domino Number Cards. Each set is made up of six index-card dominoes. Each index card, three by five inches, has dots on it for matching. The sets have matching combinations that are limited to two number configurations.

Materials:

- Thirty three-by-five-inch index cards
- Markers or crayons

- Ruler
- Stick-on dots (optional)

Directions: Make one set of six cards at a time. For each of the six cards, use the ruler to make a straight line dividing the card in half. Then make the two cards that will have doubles on them. Follow that with the four cards that will have each of the two configurations on them. For the first set, make a double of one dot. Then make a double of two dots. Then make four cards all with both one and two dots. For the second set, make a double of three dots. Then make a double of four dots. Then make four cards all with both three and four dots. Continue with this process until you have five sets of Domino Number Cards. You can make the dots with a marker or crayon or by using stick-on dots that are available in office supply stores.

How to Use and Enjoy This Toy

Use one set at a time. Play with each set twice. Start with the first set and put out the double-one-dot Domino Number Card. Then mix up the rest and put them in a pile facedown. Then take turns picking a card and matching it correctly by dots.

When all the dots are matched, put out the double-two-dot Domino Number Card. Then mix up the rest and put them in a pile facedown. As before, take turns picking a card and matching it correctly by dots.

You can play with this first set over and over as much as you and your child would like. When you feel your child is familiar with this activity and comfortable with these numbers, go on to the next set. The same rules apply to playing with each of the sets, which will go up to cards with ten dots on them.

Pick a Number

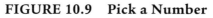

FIGURE 10.9   Pick a Number

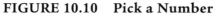

FIGURE 10.10   Pick a Number

Age Range: Eighteen Months to Three Years

Objective: To teach number recognition.

Description: A four-by-five-inch notepad with all the pages numbered in order from 1 to 10 and repeated as many times as there are pages in the book.

Materials:

- Four-by-five-inch notepad
- Marker

Directions: Write one number per page. Start with "1" and go to "10." Then repeat the sequence for as many pages as there are in the book.

How to Use and Enjoy This Toy

Take turns with your child flipping through the pages. Say the number you find on whatever page you stop. If your child does not know the number, say it. Always leave a short amount of time before you say a number for your child. If he does know it, it is better for him to say it. The surprise of finding a different number each time is what makes this activity fun.

11

Toys About Shapes

Shape Recognition

A shape is a concept that when introduced clearly can be learned at a young age. Shape Books, Shape Boxes, Shape Sorters, Shape Collections, Shape Seats, and Shape Sequences teach shapes while directly enriching your child in other areas of development—motor and language.

Shape Books

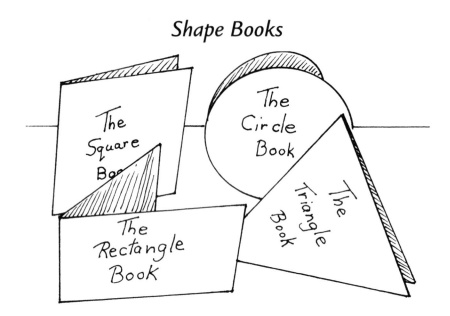

FIGURE 11.1   Shape Books

Age Range: Birth to Three Years

Objective: To teach your child recognition of shapes by repetition and familiarity.

Description: A set of file folder "books," each about a single shape. You can make as many as you wish. Circle, square, triangle, and rectangle are good for the beginning. Hexagon and oval can be next, and then you can continue with others. Each book about a shape is that shape and has pictures in it of things that are that shape.

Materials:

- One file folder (off-white or colored) for each shape
- Magazines, coloring books, or other sources of pictures
- Scissors
- White glue or paste
- Markers or crayons
- Clear contact paper or laminating material

Directions: Start with the Circle Book. Cut a folder in the shape of a circle. Be careful to leave part of the folded edge un-cut so that the folder will open like a book and not be cut into two pieces. Outline the cover with a marker and write "The Circle Book" on it. For the three remaining pages, cut out pic-tures from magazines or coloring books that have circles in them like balls, balloons, wheels, or dishes. Glue one picture on each page and write at the bottom of the page a sentence that goes with the picture like "A ball is a circle." Cover the com-pleted book with clear contact paper to protect it and make it more durable. You can also use a laminating process.

When ready to start the Square Book, cut another folder in a square, outline the cover, write "The Square Book" on it, glue in the proper pictures, and again write the appropriate descrip-tive sentences under the pictures. As before, protect it with clear contact paper or by laminating it. Use this same format and make as many Shape Books as you wish.

These are books that your child will enjoy reading over and over again. Stick with one book until you feel your child is fa-miliar with the concept. Then go ahead and introduce another. Because of all the words and sentences in these books, you will be providing for your child much language enrichment.

How to Use and Enjoy This Toy

Birth to Eighteen Months. Start with the Circle Book and use it as you would any other book with your baby. When you read it, start with the cover and say "The Circle Book." Then trace the shape with your finger or your baby's finger. Open to the first picture, point to it, and then read the descriptive sentence at the bottom. Point to each word as you read it. Use the same procedure for all the Shape Books that you make. Keep using one book until you feel your child has familiarity with the shape. When you go on to a new one, keep the others around with your child's other books to be a reminder of the shapes that he already knows.

Eighteen Months to Three Years.   Use the same reading procedure as above. However, now encourage your child to participate as much as possible in the reading process. If you feel it is appropriate for your child, you can ask him to find the shape on each page. In time, your child may want to find pictures to go into these Shape Books. He may also want to participate in making one.

Shape Boxes

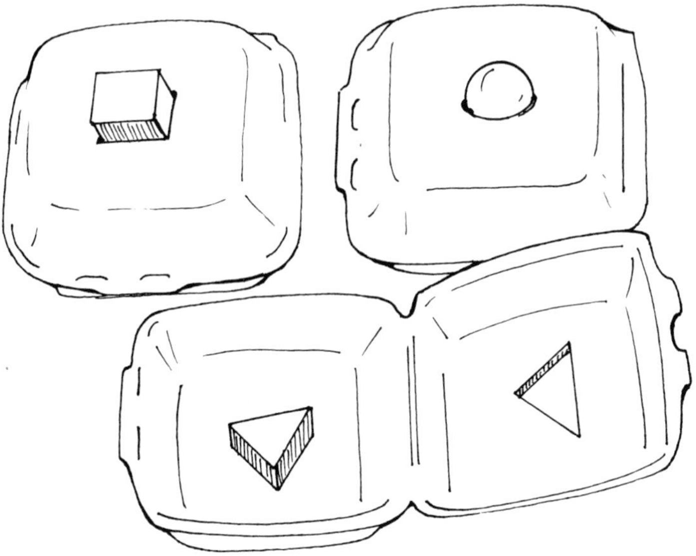

FIGURE 11.2   Shape Boxes

Age Range: Birth to Three Years

Objective: To teach your child recognition of shapes by repetition and familiarity.

Description: Plastic containers with one shape cut in each lid and one three-dimensional shape to fit in the cutout section. A suggestion is to start with a circle, square, and triangle, one in each lid. Some shapes may be difficult to find, but bottle caps from half-gallon milk or orange juice containers work well for circles, plastic or wooden blocks from block sets are handy for squares, and plastic triangle shapes from traditional shape-sorter toys or wooden blocks are popular for triangles.

Materials:

- Lidded containers
- Three-dimensional objects for circle, square, and triangle shapes

- Scissors
- Pencil

Directions: Take the lid of each container and trace the object on each lid. Then cut out each shape in the exact size of the object you traced. Put the lid back on the container and place the appropriate shape where it fits on each lid. If cut exactly to size, the shape will fit in the lid like a puzzle piece. If cut a little larger than the actual shape, it will fall through the lid into the container. Either way is okay for making this toy.

Learning the shapes in this manner is part of a hands-on approach. It is interactive and manipulative. Therefore, in addition to aiding in the learning process, this activity contributes in a major way to fine-motor development.

How to Use and Enjoy This Toy

Birth to One Year.   Start by giving your baby the Circle Shape Box. Demonstrate how the bottle cap fits into the circle cut in the lid. Help your baby place it in the lid. Because the cap is small, watch your baby carefully to make sure that he does not choke on or swallow the cap. Describe the cap as a circle as much as possible as you play. Use this Shape Box over and over until you feel your child is familiar with this circle shape. When he is ready, add the Square Shape Box. Introduce it in the same way as you did the Circle Shape Box. Then add the Triangle Shape Box when you feel it is the appropriate time.

One to Two Years.   In the beginning, use just the Circle Shape Box. Let your toddler practice putting the cap in the circle opening. Help as much or as little as is necessary. Continue to name the shape as you and your toddler play with the Circle Shape Box. When your toddler is good at that, add the Square Shape Box. Have your child place the right shape in the right box. When your child is good at discriminating between the two, add the Triangle Shape Box. As your child plays, continue to name the shape he is using.

Two to Three Years.   Now is the time for you and your child to make up your own games with these boxes. As you play, always refer to the shapes by their names.

Shape Sorters

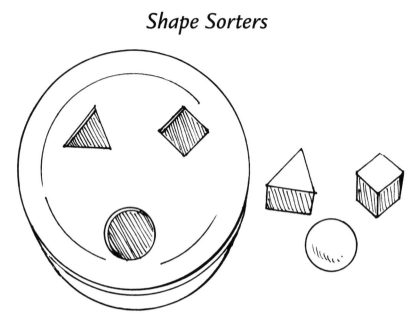

FIGURE 11.3   Shape Sorter

Age Range: Eighteen Months to Three Years

Objective: To teach your child recognition of shapes by repetition and familiarity.

Description: A lidded container with three shapes cut out in the same lid—circle, square, and triangle. Use the same shapes from the Shape Boxes described above.

Materials:

- Lidded containers
- Three-dimensional objects for circle, square, and triangle shapes
- Scissors
- Pencil

Directions: Take the lid of the container and trace the three objects on the lid. Then cut out each shape in the exact size of the object you traced. Put the lid back on the container and place the appropriate shapes where they fit in the lid. If cut exactly to size, the shapes will fit in the lid like puzzle pieces. If cut a little larger than the actual shape, they will fall through the lid into the container. Either way is okay for making this toy.

Make some additional Shape Sorters. Use lids that are large enough for two shapes. Here are some suggested combinations—just a circle and a square together, a big circle (tennis ball size) and a small circle (not too small to choke on or swallow), a big square and a small square (for two different size blocks), or some other combination of your choice.

Just as with the Shape Boxes, this hands-on approach contributes to fine-motor development. This toy with its extra pieces has even more possibilities when it comes to play.

How to Use and Enjoy This Toy

Start with the Circle, Square, and Triangle Shape Sorter toy. First, give your child the circle to place correctly. Then give him the square. Finish with the triangle. Take your turn as well and have fun with your child sorting the shapes. Then use the other Shape Sorters that you have made. Make up your own games with the big circle and the little one, the big square and the little one, or another combination that you have designed.

Shape Collections

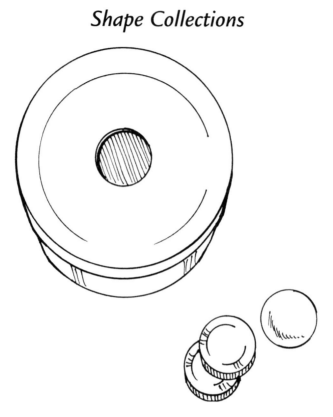

FIGURE 11.4   Shape Collection

Age Range: Eighteen Months to Three Years

Objective: To teach your child recognition of shapes by repetition and familiarity.

Description: This is one container with one lid and one circle cut in it and one container with one lid and one square cut in it. However, these containers are large enough to hold whole collections of bottle caps or blocks.

Materials:

- Two containers
- Bottle cap collection

- Block collection
- Scissors
- Pencil

Directions: Take the lid of one container and trace a bottle cap on it. Then cut out the circle shape in the exact size you traced it. Put the lid back on the container. This time cut the circle to the exact size of the bottle cap or cut it a little larger so that as you place each bottle cap through the circle in the lid, it will be able to fall through into the container.

Make another Shape Collection for blocks. Use the same procedure as above to trace the shape and cut it out. For both the Circle and the Square Collections, use containers that are large enough for your whole set of shapes.

Just as with the Shape Boxes and the Shape Sorters, Shape Collections provide a hands-on approach that contributes to fine-motor development. The repetitive activity connected with playing with a whole collection of shapes makes it a highly effective fine-motor experience.

How to Use and Enjoy This Toy

Start with the Circle Collection. One at a time, give your child a bottle cap to place correctly through the circle in the lid of the container. After that you can take your turn putting all the bottle caps through the circle. Next you can take turns putting the caps through the hole in the container. Then play with the Square Collection in the same way. Once your child is familiar with both the Circle and the Square Collections, you can mix up the bottle caps and the blocks and play a sorting game. Be sure to take your turn as you play. After that make up your own games with these Shape Collections.

Shape Seats

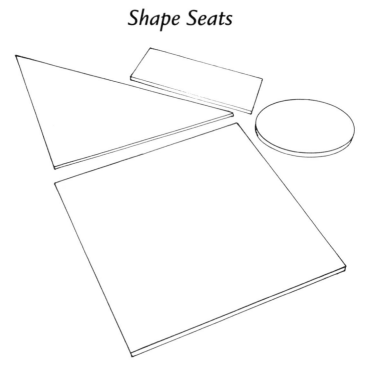

FIGURE 11.5   Shape Seats

Age Range: Birth to Three Years

Objective: To teach your child recognition of shapes by repetition and familiarity.

Description: Four large shapes cut out of two large pieces of oak tag. There should be a complete laminated set of a circle, square, triangle, and rectangle in red, yellow, blue, and green.

Materials:

- Eight large pieces of oak tag in red, yellow, blue, and green, about twenty-eight by twenty-four inches, two in each color
- Laminating material

- Ruler
- Scissors
- Pencil

Directions: Start with the first red sheet. Measure a square in it about twenty-two inches square. Cut out the square, and you will already have a rectangle. Take the second red sheet. Repeat the same process. This time divide the square in half diagonally and cut it into a triangle. Using the second triangle, cut a circle in it about twelve inches in diameter. A good way to find a pattern is to use a ten-inch plate as a form to trace. Then you can cut the shape to be two inches wider all around. Besides a plate, you might have a bowl or serving platter that you can trace. Once you have all four shapes cut, take them to be laminated.

When you have your circle, square, triangle, and rectangle complete, follow the same procedure for making the yellow shapes. Then move on to the blue and then the green. Once you have completed making all the shapes, you will have each shape in each of the four colors.

These large-size shapes will be very effective for making an impression on your child about the shapes. Because they are appropriate for so many different free-form activities, you will find that they will generate a lot of conversation. All of this creative play will play a role in stimulating your child's language development.

How to Use and Enjoy This Toy

Birth to One Year.   Start with the set of red shapes. First, give your baby the red circle. It is a nice, stiff card and in a very attractive color for babies. Be sure to identify it as a circle whenever you see your baby looking at it. When you feel your baby is familiar with the circle, add the square to his play area. He can sit on either one of these as well. Next come the triangle and then the rectangle. After you have used the red shapes many times, go on to the yellow ones, then the blue, and then the green.

One to Two Years.   Give your toddler all four circles for play. You can do many things with these. They can be seats. They can also mark play stations. You can set up groups of toys that are the same color as the circle and put them near that circle. Use these four colored circles in any creative way that you wish. After sufficient exposure to the circles, make up some activities with the squares. Then use the triangles and then the rectangles.

Two to Three Years.   Take out the whole set of red shapes and use them in any way you wish. Your two-year-old will probably give you many ideas. You can use these as the kickoff for having a whole red day—using other red toys and even dressing in that color. Play with each of the color groups separately and enjoy all your new ideas. Next you might want to add a second group of shapes like the yellow ones. With two colors, you might want to set up a matching activity of shapes that match each other. There may be times you might want to use all the shapes in all the colors. Use and enjoy your Shape Seats in your own special way.

Shape Sequences

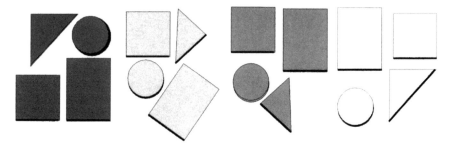

FIGURE 11.6   Shape Sequences

Age Range: Birth to Three Years

Objective: To teach your child recognition of shapes by repetition and familiarity.

Description: A set of small shape cards, a miniature version of Shape Seats. You will have four small shapes cut out of one standard-size piece of construction paper. There should be a complete laminated set of a circle, square, triangle, and rectangle in red, yellow, blue, and green.

Materials:

- Four regular-size pieces of construction paper in red, yellow, blue, and green, nine by twelve inches
- Laminating material
- Ruler
- Scissors
- Pencil

Directions: Start with the red sheet. Fold it in quarters and then cut it into quarters. In one quarter, trace a circle from a twelve-ounce old-fashioned-size glass. You may have another type of glass that will serve as a good template for tracing. In the next quarter, cut out a square. Since one side of the paper is four and a half inches wide, cut the other side to the same length, and you will have a square. Take another quarter, cut that one also into a square, and then cut it diagonally to make a triangle. The fourth will be a ready-made rectangle. Next take a yellow sheet. Go through the same steps again. After that repeat the procedure with the blue and green sheets of paper. Once you have all four colored sheets cut into all four shapes, take all sixteen shapes to be laminated. Four of these shapes will fit on a standard-size laminating sheet. Cut them apart after they are laminated. This should turn out to be a quick and easy job.

Just as with the large shapes, these small shapes will be very effective for making an impression on your child about the shapes. Both the sequencing activities and the different ways you will find yourselves playing with the cards will generate a lot of conversation. All of these activities will play a role in stimulating your child's language development.

How to Use and Enjoy This Toy

Birth to One Year.   First, give your baby the red circle. Just as with the large shapes, this will be a stiff, interesting texture and in a very attractive color. Be sure to identify it as a circle whenever you see your baby looking at it. When you feel your baby is familiar with the circle, add the red square to his play area. Next, add the triangle and then the rectangle. After you have used the red shapes many times, go on to the yellow ones, then the blue, and then the green. Use the colors separately to make the greatest impact.

One to Two Years.   Give your toddler all four small circles for play. You can do many things with these. You can set up the red, yellow, and green circles to look like a traffic light. You can also make interesting designs with them. Another idea is to set out a circle, square, triangle, and rectangle in one color and then set out the other colored shapes in the same way. You can also set out a shape like a square in each of the colors and sort all the other shapes in that way. Your toddler can also be your guide as he constructs his own shape activities. Use these many colored shapes in any creative way that you wish.

Two to Three Years.   You can begin making patterns with these shapes. Start off very simple. You could do something like red, yellow, red, yellow, and more. You could also do circle, square, circle, square, circle, square, and circle, square. Have fun as you create patterns that seem appropriate for your own child. Help as much or as little as is necessary.

12

Toys About Reading

Reading Development

After having had the experience of teaching reading to first-graders, I decided that maybe it would be easier and more natural to learn to read while learning to talk. Knowing the complicated phonics rules we teach, that so many words break those rules, and that someone who knows how to read rarely if ever sounds out a word, I was looking for a better way.

After years of research, Dr. O. K. Moore of Yale University had some supportive results. As reported in *How to Teach Your Baby to Read* by Glenn Doman, he found that it was easier to teach a three-year-old to read than a four-year-old, a four-year-old than a five-year-old, and a five-year-old than a six-year-old.

The principle behind the approach I developed is the same as the one a baby uses when learning to identify pictures. First the baby learns that a specific picture is a duck. Then the baby recognizes more and more pictures as ducks. Finally, the baby can recognize any duck, no matter what size, shape, or color it is. In this case, the baby first learns the word in large letters on colored paper and in time can identify it in any size and in any handwriting or print.

This whole process stems from the process of learning to talk. Knowing the meaning of his words, he can actually learn to read while he is learning to talk. The written word gives the spoken word another dimension. As your child says his first words, he can see their written representations.

Word Books

FIGURE 12.1   Word Books

Age Range: One to Three Years

Objective: To teach your child to read through personal iden-
tification with specific words.

Description: Five three-ring folders each labeled "Book" on
the front and having different-colored copy paper inside with a
different word in large print on each page.

Materials:

- Five three-ring folders (start with five and add more as you
  need them)
- Copy paper—fifty multicolored sheets, eight and a half by
  eleven inches in size
- Hole puncher
- Marker or crayon

Directions: Three-hole-punch the colored copy paper so that it will fit in the folders. Fill each folder with ten multicolored sheets of paper. These pages will not be durable, and they may rip easily. However, if they do, they are very easy to replace. Start with one book and make more as you need them. Print the word "Book" on the cover of the folder. On the first page, print one of the first words your child has learned to say. Print this word and all others that follow with a dark-colored marker or crayon in large, clear letters. Begin the first letter of each word with a capital letter and make the rest lowercase. It might seem that writing in all capitals would be easier to read, but it makes no difference. It is better to use lowercase because that is what is used in books. Start with one word in a book and add others as your child begins to have fun saying other words.

How to Use and Enjoy This Toy

One to Two Years.   When you hear your child saying a word with a big smile and enjoying it, show him the word in the book. Your toddler will like seeing the written form of the word. When the book has only one page with a word printed on it, have him read it that way. As you add individual words to other pages, your child will be reading a longer book. The reason the words are presented on pages in a book labeled "Book" and not on cards is to give the idea that words are written in books.

Fill up each book word by word. Record in these books all new words that your child learns to say. You will probably be successful capturing about the first fifty words. Then you will have a nice collection of five books with ten words in each one. These are books that you make as you go along and personalize to your own child's vocabulary. You cannot buy any other books that have these special qualities.

Two to Three Years.   You can continue making more word books like these. You can also make books that have two-word combinations that your baby now says. You might eventually want to include short phrases that your child likes to say. Keep these books around for your child to enjoy. Then he will be able to pick them up anytime and enjoy the independence and satisfaction of being able to read his own special books.

Word Notebook

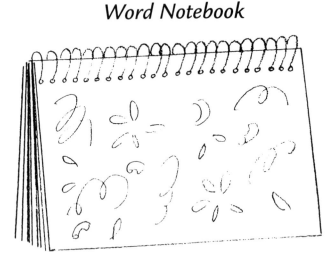

FIGURE 12.2   Word Notebook

FIGURE 12.3   Word Notebook

Age Range: Two to Three Years

Objective: To teach your child to read by repetition and familiarity of pleasant words.

Description: A four-by-six-inch spiral-bound index-card notebook with familiar words in it from your child's Word Books. It can also have new words or phrases.

Materials:

- Four-by-six-inch spiral-bound index-card notebook
- Crayon

Directions: Using a crayon on the lined sides of the cards, print favorite words from the Word Books, one word per page, in the four-by-six-inch spiral-bound index-card notebook. This will show your child that he can read some of his words in another place. The more different places he sees them, the sooner he will be able to read them anywhere. You will probably see this first with his name and words like "Mommy" and "Daddy." Add words to the book one at a time. Make sure he knows one before entering another. When he starts to say phrases or sentences, you can use this book to introduce them one at a time. You can decorate the front of the book by putting a label on it or some designs or stickers. In this way, you will be making this book more appealing to your child.

How to Use and Enjoy This Toy

One to Two Years.   When you are waiting in line somewhere with your child, in a doctor's office or in a restaurant, you can keep him happily amused with this personalized reading book. It will have words in it he likes to say, and he will enjoy saying them when shown a particular word, phrase, or sentence. The spiral-bound notebook allows you to start with one word and gradually expand your book. No specific number of words is needed. The right number is the number that you have built over time. Your toddler will probably open this book up to different pages each time. That is the surprise quality that adds to the fun and also contributes to the effectiveness of the teaching.

Two to Three Years.   Continue adding words and phrases as you were doing before. This time ask your child for favorite words or phrases. He will then enjoy reading many of these over and over. Remember to make entries in this book one at a time and not to add new ones until your child has had enough repetition with the old ones to be very familiar with them. Just as before, your child can read the words, phrases, and sentences in this book in any order. Whatever page he opens it up to is fine.

Categories Book

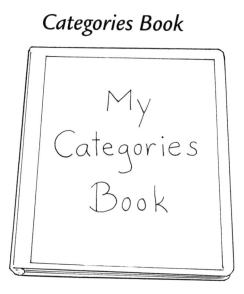

FIGURE 12.4 Categories Book

FIGURE 12.5 Categories Book

Age Range: Birth to Three Years

Objective: To teach your child to read through meaningful associations.

Description: A three-ring binder filled with five colors of copy paper, six sheets of each color, in three-hole-punched plastic sleeves. The first page of each color has a category name like "Flowers," "Animals," "People," "Toys," and "Food" printed on it in large, clear letters. The next five pages each contain one picture from that category and a word or words to describe it.

Materials:

- One-inch three-ring binder
- Thirty sheets of copy paper, six each of five different colors
- Thirty sheets of three-hole-punched plastic page protectors
- Magazines, catalogs, greeting cards, or other sources of pictures
- Scissors
- White glue or paste
- Marker

Directions: Place each one of the thirty sheets of colored copy paper in a three-hole plastic page protector. Place the thirty protected pages in the one-inch binder, keeping the pages separated into groups by color. Write each category on the first sheet of each color and leave the following four sheets blank, ready for pictures in that category. For example, if the first category is "Flowers" on pink paper, write only the word "Flowers" on the first pink page and then glue or paste pictures of flowers cut from magazines, greeting cards, or other sources on each of the next four pink pages. Place one picture on each page and print one word or several words under each to name the picture. If you find lots of pictures that you like for any one category, you can add more pages to that category. This is a book that you can build over time. Boxes are a good source of easily accessible pictures. Boxes from toys have colorful pictures of the toy that you can cut out for the "Toys" category. Boxes from crackers or cereal will often have good pictures for the "Food" category, and many toy and food boxes have attractive pictures of infants, toddlers, and young children on them that would be great for the "People" category.

How to Use and Enjoy This Toy

Birth to Eighteen Months.   Read this book with your baby much as you have done with the other picture books you have made. Point to the picture and describe it with the word or words under it and then point to the word or words under it and read them. You are showing your baby that the picture and the words are the same. In this way, you are introducing some sight words in the context of an interesting picture book for your baby. By repetition and familiarity your child will be learning to read.

Eighteen Months to Three Years.   Now that your toddler is familiar with many of these pictures and words, he will be able to participate more in the reading process. As you point to the pictures and words, leave time for your child to say as many of the words as he can. In addition, together look through magazines, catalogs, greeting cards, and other sources of pictures to find new entries for your Categories Book. Cut them out and glue or paste them on new pages together. Having your child contribute to part of the creative process for this book will make it even more meaningful to him.

Picture Cards

FIGURE 12.6   Picture Cards

Age Range: Eighteen Months to Three Years

Objective: To teach reading by enhancing visual discrimination skills.

Description: Five matching sets of picture postcards.

Materials: Five matching sets of picture postcards.

Directions: Put together a set of ten postcards, five sets of two matching pictures each.

How to Use and Enjoy This Toy

Eighteen Months to Three Years.   Start by showing your toddler two cards that match. Then show your toddler two more. Then place two different ones out on the table. Take turns matching the other two cards. When your child is familiar with this process, introduce a third set to this activity. Again, when your child is ready, introduce the fourth and then the fifth set. Take turns matching one card at a time and then eventually matching the whole set.

Keep this postcard matching game in mind when you are out. Either with or without your child, collect as many postcard matches as you can. Organize them in sets of ten when you get them. In addition, because the pictures will be about places you have been and some where your child has been as well, these cards will be a stimulus for interesting and enjoyable conversations.

Healthy Eating Cards

FIGURE 12.7   Healthy Eating Cards

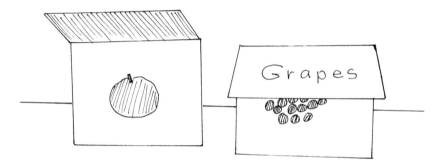

FIGURE 12.8   Healthy Eating Cards

Age Range: Eighteen Months to Three Years

Objective: To teach reading by associating words to pictures.

Description: Five-by-eight-inch index cards folded in half. A word like "Apple," "Banana," or "Oatmeal" is written on the outside; a fruit, vegetable, or whole grain food is pictured on the inside.

Materials: Five-by-eight-inch index cards, unlimited number

Directions: One by one, fold a five-by-eight-inch index card in half. Write a word for a fruit, vegetable, or whole-grain food on the front of the card. Examples are "Tomato," "Broccoli," and "Pasta." Draw a picture with crayons of the matching food on the inside.

Besides teaching reading, these cards teach what kinds of foods are nutritious. Natural foods that are not processed and do not have artificial colors, flavors, or preservatives are ones that you should draw for this activity. Refer to Chapter 1 for helpful information about nutrition.

Children love rainbows. Healthy eating means eating natural foods from all the colors of the rainbow—purple, red, orange, yellow, blue, and green. Here are some ideas for teaching your child how to eat across the rainbow:

- Purple—grapes, plums
- Red—apples, strawberries
- Orange—Oranges, carrots
- Brown—Cereal, bread
- Yellow—Bananas, lemons
- Blue—Blueberries
- Green—Spinach, green beans

How to Use and Enjoy This Toy

Put out a set of Healthy Eating Cards that you have made. Pick a card and show it to your child. See if he can tell from the word what the picture will be when you open the card. If he was not able to say the word before you opened the card, show him the word afterward and see if he is willing to say it then. Repeat this activity with as many different Healthy Eating Cards as you like. Play as long as you both stay interested in the activity.

Building on the rainbow idea, you can arrange your Healthy Eating Cards into color categories. Be sure to emphasize that foods with the most nutrients are ones with deep, beautiful colors. You may also want to include white milk and black blackberries as nutritious foods with true colors. This is a wonderful time to introduce to your child the concept of healthy eating and to talk about it and explain it as well.

Word Cards

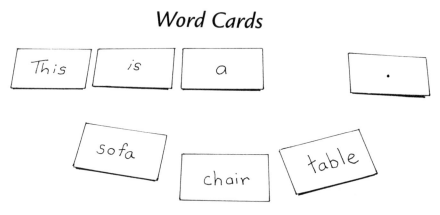

FIGURE 12.9   Word Cards

Age Range: Two to Three Years

Objective: To teach reading by labeling items around the house.

Description: A set of twenty-five three-by-five-inch index cards with labels on them including word cards for "This," "is," "a," and one for a period. The beginning activity starts with three label cards and is expanded to include more labels a little at a time.

Materials:

- Twenty-five three-by-five-inch index cards
- Marker

Directions: Start with making three labels. Suggested words are "sofa," "table," and "chair." Then add cards for "This," "is," "a," and one for a period. Make additional labels when your child is familiar with the first three.

How to Use and Enjoy This Toy

Set out on a table the word cards "This," "is," and "a." Then place three labels in appropriate places in the room. Then have fun with these sentence cards. Together with your child, select label cards to complete the sentence. Take turns finding labels and putting them in the right place in the sentence and then adding the period at the end. Make and use the new labels when you feel your child is ready.

Word Puzzles

FIGURE 12.10   Word Puzzles

Age Range: One to Three Years

Objective: To teach reading by creating a puzzle activity.

Description: White construction-paper sheets with words and pictures on them, two of each picture. One is cut into appropriate-size puzzle pieces and the other remains intact as a guide for putting the puzzle back together. Both the whole version and the cut version are held together for storage by a large paper clip or in a nine-by-twelve-inch envelope with the appropriate words on it.

Materials:

- Twelve sheets of nine-by-twelve-inch white construction paper

- Marker
- Crayons
- Scissors
- Clear contact paper or laminating material
- Large paper clip or nine-by-twelve-inch envelope

Directions: On sheets of white construction paper, print with a marker a word, a two-word phrase, or a three-word phrase. Examples are your child's name, "My house," and "I love you." Then color with crayons a border or pictures that go with the words. For each sheet that you make, make a duplicate. On the back of one in each pair, draw with a pencil lines to cut the picture apart into puzzle pieces. Design it as three pieces for your one-year-old and four for your two-year-old. Before you actually cut the puzzle pieces, cover both parts of the pair with clear contact paper or laminate them. Use a large paper clip to keep the model sheet and the cut sheet together or place the model and its pieces in a nine-by-twelve-inch envelope with the word label on the outside.

How to Use and Enjoy This Toy

One to Two Years.   Have fun with your toddler putting the three-piece puzzles together. Help as much or as little as is necessary.

Two to Three Years.   Have fun with your two-year-old putting the four-piece puzzles together. Help as much or as little as is necessary.

Record a Book

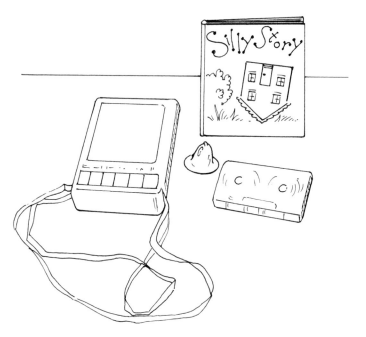

FIGURE 12.11   **Record a Book**

Age Range: One to Three Years

Objective: To teach reading through connecting auditory and visual discrimination.

Description: A book of your choice and your voice recording the book.

Materials:

- Book of your choice
- Tape recorder
- Blank cassette tape
- Bell, squeaker, or pencil

Directions: Select a book that your child likes. Recommended is a board book with durable pages. Follow this procedure for making your recording. Start by saying the title and the author. Then explain that you are going to read the book and will make a certain sound like a bell or a squeaker or will tap on the table with a pencil when it is time to turn the page. Then tell your child to open the book to the first page. Begin reading.

How to Use and Enjoy This Toy

One to Two Years.   Have a baby-sitter or whoever stays with your toddler when you are away set up the book and tape for your child. Have this person help your child with this activity as much as necessary.

Two to Three Years.   Teach your child to be able to use this book and tape as independently as possible. As mentioned above, give as much help as is necessary for your child to be able to master this process.

Part THREE

The Endless Learning Process

13

Follow-Up Activities

Ages Three to Five Years

The focus of this book is on activities for infants and toddlers, but the ideas can be applied to your child as he continues to grow. I hope that knowledge of how to make personalized educational toys and books, how to use what you have made, and how to stimulate and direct your child through his daily routine will aid you as you continue to make toys for your child. The following are suggestions for follow-up activities in each of the areas—self-awareness, colors, letters, numbers, shapes, and reading.

Self-Awareness

Try to set up for your child somewhere in the house a small house and a small store to which he can go and take charge.

FIGURE 13.1   The Pantry House and Store

Look for a place at the bottom of a closet or pantry or convert a corner in a bedroom or playroom. Sometimes a big carton can isolate the space. Having enough room is always a problem, but rearranging can often free up a new area.

Here is what one mother said: "In our house my daughter always used to go under the bottom shelf of our pantry. My husband would say, 'There she goes into her little house.' One day it clicked, and I designed her space into 'her little house.' I decorated the walls with brightly colored contact paper. I did not peel the back completely, only in enough spots to make it stick, because peeling the whole back of such a large sheet would make it difficult to apply without bubbles and creases. It became a place where she could keep her dolls, some dishes, a broom and dustpan, and other playhouse items.

"Because I was lucky enough to have room to give up the first shelf of my pantry, she soon had a store. I took another color of contact paper to do the walls, made a wrapping paper awning (protected with clear contact paper), and a short cardboard double door. One side of the store was decorated as shelves for the boxes. The other side had a picture of a refrigerator for egg cartons, milk and ice-cream containers, and other packaging from refrigerator items. In the middle was a rectangular plastic money box. It had a place for index-card dollar bills on one side and a small paper cup on the other for play money coins. Instead of throwing out a box, I put a price tag on it made from stick-on dots and placed it in the store. I tried to price the items rounded to about what they cost in a store. My daughter loves to play store with anyone who comes to visit. She gives them the money first. They ask to buy something. She finds it, tells the price, gives the item, collects the money, and places it correctly in her money box. As she develops a better command of numbers, I will leave the original prices on the boxes."

Colors

If they have worked for you, continue with Follow-Up Color Boxes and Follow-Up Color Books. This time use different-size containers for the new colors, such as pink, purple, orange, brown, black, and white. By using easy-to-handle containers, you also will have created a stacking toy.

To make more books and put them together even more quickly, you can use construction-paper pages for the whole book and staple it together. If you do it that way, cover the staple binding with several layers of masking tape to prevent cuts from the staples. Because your child is a little older, these books may not need durable covers like what was needed for the first four Color Books. If you would like to make a Silver Book, try tinfoil over cardboard for all the pages, even the cover. In addition, cover all the pages with clear contact paper or laminate

FIGURE 13.2   Lowercase Letter Cards

them. Exposed tinfoil is dangerous because it could crumble, and your child could swallow it by mistake.

Letters

Once your child has mastered the capital letters, you can go on to the Lowercase Letter Cards. Take a small pack of file box dividers about three by five inches. They already have the capital check letter on one side. On the side of each card opposite the check letter, write the corresponding lowercase letter.

Using one card at a time, show the lowercase letter and quickly the capital on the back naming them both the same each time you show each one. Repeat this a few times. Then show the lowercase and have your child try to say it before you turn over the capital check letter. If he does not say it right away, show it. Let him know he is not wrong, just not fast enough to say it before you showed it; in time he will be. Although the emphasis of the game is on being able to say the lowercase letter fast enough (before you show the capital letter) and not on being right or wrong, learning is taking place.

The ABC Song has for generations been a natural way that children have learned the alphabet. Using small stick-on letters or a crayon or marker on a simple sheet of construction paper, set up the alphabet to the rhythm of the actual song. Now when you sing this song with your child, you will have a place to point to the letters at the same time. This will help your child connect the sounds he hears with the visual representation of the letters. This is a very good way to clear up the confusion about the word "and" in the song. You can also write the popular ending as shown.

Numbers

Take a three-by-five-inch spiral-bound index-card notebook. Put a label on the front cover or decorate it with stickers or some other design to make it look more appealing to your child. Use the lined side of the cards (if one side has lines) and write the numbers to 100 by tens. When your child can recognize those, use the remaining pages in the book to write the numbers to 100 by fives.

When he seems to know how to recognize the numbers by fives and tens, start a section with numbers from 11 to 20. Then move on to 21 to 30. That should do it for Follow-Up Number Book 1.

If you and your child are enjoying this number book process, start Follow-Up Number Book 2. Here are some suggestions for that book: 31–40, 41–50, 51–60, 61–70, and 71–80.

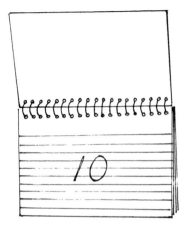

FIGURE 13.3   Follow-Up Number Book I

FIGURE 13.4   Follow-Up Number Book I

If all is still going well, go ahead and make another Number Book. Continue with 81–90 and 91–100. Then, if your child is still with you, add numbers from 101 to 110. Then you can top this book off with numbers that should be great fun for your child: 100, 200, 300, 400, and on up to 1,000. You will then have ten pages left. Use them as you wish.

With all of these books, be sure to introduce each new number sequence when you sense your child is ready for it. This

FIGURE 13.5   Follow-Up Number Book II

FIGURE 13.6   Follow-Up Number Book II

process is not a race. This is a process to be enjoyed over time. Much of the learning will come from your child's continued opportunity to look through this interesting homemade book that you have made for him number by number.

At the same time you are making and using these books, you can point out speed limit signs when you are in the car driving by. While in the car, you can say something like, "I see a number on that sign. It is _____." Say the number if your child does not say

FIGURE 13.7   Follow-Up Shape Book

it. In the beginning, you will always say the number before your child does. Later he will be able to recognize it before you say it.

Numbers are everywhere. Your child may especially like to call them out as they light up in an elevator. He might also like to find them as they mark the aisles in a supermarket. The more that you can point out to a young child, the more he will learn. All of this information and recognition will add meaning to his environment. It will actually heighten his awareness.

Shapes

If you had success with the Shape Books, this is a good time to make a Follow-Up Shape Book. In this one, you can use dividers to label different shapes. Then you and your child can enjoy finding objects in different shapes and pasting them on the proper pages.

Shapes are everywhere, and your child may begin to notice them in his environment. There are many squares and rectangles in houses, and look how many circles (wheels) make the world go 'round! Moreover, tiles today are full of interesting shapes. There is no reason not to point out the popular pentagon seen on every soccer ball.

A great idea is to become shape detectives when waiting together in a new place. You might be in a room waiting for a doctor to see you. It could be a restaurant or some other place of interest. To pass the time, take turns identifying circles, squares, triangles, and rectangles in the room. Soon you will notice details on lamps, dressers, cabinets, and other items that you have never noticed before. This pleasant pastime will probably turn out to be quite interesting, enjoyable, and educational.

Reading

Word cards in a file box will make a very good beginning for many of the follow-up activities that you can do. Use three-by-five-inch index cards and a file box made for cards that size. You can store all kinds of word cards in a Word Card File Box. Use either a marker or a crayon to write the words.

You can make one set of cards that are just nouns. These can be labels. Write them on one color of index cards. Here are some suggested starter words: "Door," "Lamp," "Desk," "Carpet," and "Pillow." Write each one on a card and go over them with your child. Then put them in the proper places in the room. Take them away and have your child try to do it. After he becomes good at those five, add a new word each time you play. A variation of this activity is to take them from their proper places and mix them up. Then have your child put them back in their proper places. For both of these activities you can take your turn, and you can also help as much as is needed in the process.

You can make another set of cards that are just verbs. These can be actions. Write them on another color. Again, start with about five words like "Walk," "Clap," "Hop," "Jump," and "Sing." Write each word on a card and go over them with your

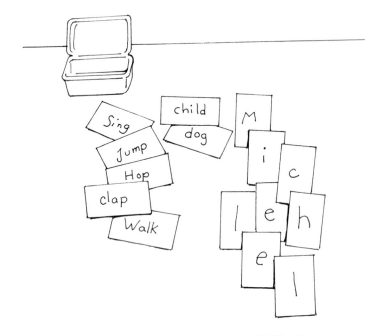

FIGURE 13.8   Word Card File Box

child. Then take turns with your child picking a card and doing the action on it. After he is familiar with all five, add a new one each time you play. A variation of this activity is to take turns doing all the actions on all the cards and then watching the other person do them as well.

Suggested is to use index cards in one color for nouns and in another color for verbs. That will help you to keep them separate.

Favorite words can be added to this activity as well. From time to time ask your child to give you a favorite. Then you can add it to either the noun or the verb collection.

Early reading can also benefit speech. You can collect words on cards that will help your child to say those words more clearly. Here are some examples that have been helpful to many children. You might want to use another color for these words.

- Dell—This is the word "dell" from the song "The Farmer in the Dell." Since many children and even adults do not know what it means, they often say it incorrectly. If you write it out on one of your word cards, you will help your child to say it more clearly. Defined in *Webster's New World Dictionary*, it means "a small, secluded valley or glen, usually wooded" (p. 159).
- Chest—This is the word "chest" from the song "John Brown's Baby." Since many children who sing that song are not familiar with that word, they often say it as "dressed" or something similar to that. If you write it out on one of your word cards, you will see what a difference it will make.

Every parent has a favorite story about a word or words his child has said wrong because he did not know the meaning. Usually these situations come up in relation to a word or words in a song or rhyme. One mother laughed as she said her four-year-old recited the Pledge of Allegiance saying, ". . . and to Publix in the sand."

Switch now to another color of index cards and have some fun unscrambling words. Count off as many cards as are necessary for each letter of your child's name. Then, holding the cards in the vertical position, begin writing the name with a capital letter and then write one letter per card. Mix up the letters and then put them out in front of your child. Let your child unscramble the cards to spell his name correctly. Help as little or as much as is necessary. If this game is a hit with your child, take more colored index cards and unscramble some other names. Suggested are your name, your child's middle and last names, names of other family members, names of your child's friends, and friends of the family.

Continuing with the cards idea, you can set up a new file box to be a Mailbox. Suggested for this activity are four-by-six-inch

FIGURE 13.9   Mailbox

cards. Depending on the reading vocabulary of your child, write one-, two-, three-, or four-word messages and leave them in your child's Mailbox at least once a day. When your child is ready, write action messages from which you will be able to see actual results. For example, "Open the window." "Bring me a book." "Hug your mom."

With the same four-by-six-inch cards, create an active Directions Game. Write simple directions on a set of cards, one sentence per card. Then take turns picking a card and following the direction. Keep the sentence to three or four words. If your child has trouble reading any of the words, help as much as you can. Here are some popular directions. "Close the door." "Tie your shoe." "Clap your hands." "Jump three times." "Walk around the table."

Keep going with the four-by-six-inch cards and set up some Treasure Hunts. Hide some small prizes in different parts of your

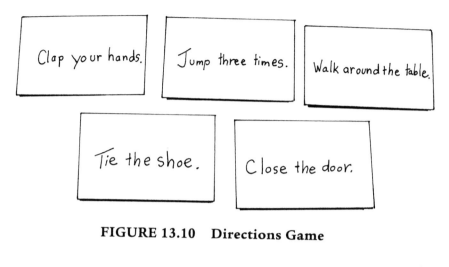

FIGURE 13.10   Directions Game

FIGURE 13.11   Treasure Hunts

house. Examples of prizes are a box of crayons, a package of stickers, an orange or banana with a face drawn on the skin with a nontoxic marker, play putty, and a small ball (not small enough to swallow). Then set up three clues for each prize. Here is a sample set of clues. "Look under the table." "Go to the sink." "Look behind the curtain."

Once your child becomes interested in reading, you will find many avenues for finding words to read. One favorite is words in the titles in newspapers, magazines, and catalogs. Here are a few words that are quite common. "Open," "the," "window," "to," "world," "summer," "fall," "winter," "spring," "best," "new," "and," "shoes," "fun," "tips," "food," "this," "live," "at," "men," "women," "great," "gift," "for," "life," "health," "family," "can," "your," "right," "fat," and "you." There are many more. Another great place to look is on food boxes. Here you will find words like "salt," "sugar," "flour," "milk," "soy," "rice," "oats," "cereal," and "crackers." In addition, signs are everywhere and can become an interesting and meaningful part of your child's environment. Start to point out "Stop," "Exit," "One Way," "Open," "No Parking" and more. They provide built-in repetition.

Just as learning to talk is a natural process, so is learning to read. Once you hear your baby say his first word, you know many more will follow. It is the same with reading. Once you observe your child reading his first word, many more will follow. The key factor for a child learning to talk is exposure to a rich language environment—a high quality and high quantity of language modeled with correct grammar. Similarly, the key for learning to read is exposure to many words that are clearly written. Words that are repeated will help your child become familiar with them and will aid in the speed and effectiveness of learning to read them.

This book is about teaching with toys. Toys are vehicles for play. Play is about having fun. Reading is great fun. It will bring your child information and satisfaction. It is totally positive. When people ask you why you are teaching reading to your young child, you will be able to share with them that you are doing it through play. Remember to stop the activity if it becomes tedious or problematic in any other way. Remember also to keep that spirit of play with you as you do any of the reading activities.

14

Putting It All Together

Educational Stimulation and the Big Picture

According to what we know in the twenty-first century about child development, children need to experience a specific kind of environment to thrive. Here are the five elements that they need.

- Nurturing love
- Guidance
- Support
- Protection
- Educational stimulation

Each one alone is important, and together they are a must.

Dr. Burton White

Burton White was the first one to identify the five elements children need in 1975. At that time he reported them to the nation in his landmark book called *The First Three Years of Life*. His research question was "What is it about the lives of children who are successful when they start school that is different from the children who are not?" In today's terms we would substitute the words "successful when they start school" for "ready for school." After thirty years of research, he found out that it was what happens to children in their first three years. He tells us that if children are well developed by the time they are three years old, they will automatically be predictive of being successful in school at age six.

He did not leave us hanging even a little bit about how children can become well developed. As part of his research, he was able to identify the above categories of experiences for children to have during the years from birth to age three to become well developed.

In his book he explained exactly what experiences are necessary as part of those categories. Since 1975 many a parent has read his book to learn about what experiences to provide for their children in the first three years so that their children will be well developed by age three and correspondingly predictive of being successful in school at age six.

As you near the end of *Baby and Toddler Learning Fun*, you will realize that all of that information is assembled in this book in a way that is easy to follow. This book is unique because it not only tells you what you need to do during the first three years, but it also tells you exactly how to do it. New research reports a lack of nurturing love, guidance, support, and educational stimulation as the cause of crime and violence. It traces it right back to the infant, toddler, and two-year-old stages.

With this book, you are holding these qualities in your hands. As you live the process, remember that you are taking your step against crime and violence. How incredible it is that it is so simple, so much fun, and that it works.

Part 1 of this book is all about what to do. It explains everything. Look how the chapters line up with the first four basic concepts.

- Chapter 1, "Toys, Play, and Learning": This is all about nurturing love.
- Chapter 2, "Why Make Your Own Toys?": This is all about guidance.
- Chapter 3, "Toy-Making Workshops": This is all about support.
- Chapter 4, "Collecting Developmental Ideas": This is all about protection.
- Chapter 5, "Collecting Daily Tips": This is more about protection.

Taken together, all these chapters lead you through a full program of educational stimulation. Then Part 2 tells you exactly how to do it. You learn how to make and use toys in five areas.

Nurturing Love

Chapter 1, "Toys, Play, and Learning," tells you about spending time with your little one. It tells you how important this relationship-building time is. You find out about music, about homemade toys, about the power of repetition and familiarity, about how natural it is to be with your child, about uniqueness, about simplicity, curiosity, and spontaneity. The family, home, and parenting turn out to be center stage.

Guidance

Chapter 2, "Why Make Your Own Toys?" tells you what toys you need to guide your child. Lo and behold, they are simple. In addition, they are creative. Both you and your child will feel alive from the process. If you could buy all the toys you need, that would be one thing; but you really cannot. This process is about pitching in, interacting, and creating.

Support

Chapter 3, "Toy-Making Workshops," is all about support. The basic premise is for parents to support each other. It is that support that will help you provide the necessary support for your own child. During these workshops you share ideas, information, and even supplies. You learn how to teach your child appropriately and the all-important concept that "Every minute, every hour, every day is important in the life of a child."

Protection

Chapter 4, "Collecting Developmental Ideas," zeroes in at the heart of protection. In one way, everyone who becomes a parent knows exactly how to take care of his or her baby. That is the way nature meant it to be. However, on the other hand, this is something that is passed on from grandparents to parents and not originally set up as part of a hectic fast-paced world. Therefore, here you learn about the newest and most up-to-date resources to help you provide the most optimal environment for your own child. When you get done with this chapter, you will have a good understanding of development in five areas and how to facilitate it as well.

Chapter 5, "Collecting Daily Tips," is a continuation of protection. First you get a solid overview from a practical standpoint of nutrition, exercise, and sleep. This is the triangle of health. After that you get ideas for self-help, play, and other miscellaneous advice. You can see how the concept of protection grows in different ways.

Educational Stimulation

That is what you find in this whole book. You have every important route and reference for providing for your child in the first three years a strong educational foundation. At the end, you have follow-up activities that help you help your child as he progresses to the preschool years during the ages of three to five years.

Your Important Role

In today's technological society it is easy to start to think that you and your presence are not particularly important to your child. However, as a safeguard against that kind of thinking, I share this education story with you. One group of preschool teachers took their children out to play on a playground. They all sat together on a bench and enjoyed their time chatting with each other. One by one each child came over to them and complained about another child hitting or fighting with them. Another group of preschool teachers took their children to the playground and they all split up monitoring a different part of the play area. As play proceeded, not one child missed even five seconds of play to experience or complain about any kind of unpleasant experience.

As you think about toys and teaching your child, keep the following goals in mind:

1. To fill your home environment with those things you want your child to learn.
2. To use household materials that you otherwise might have thrown out.

Keeping these goals in mind will help you continue to provide meaningful toys for your child. Repetition, familiarity, and stimulating the five senses can be a guide for you for making and using interesting educational toys for your child.

Appendix

Appendix A Workshop Worksheet for Self-Awareness

	List Materials Assembled	Date Project Completed
My Name Toy		Jan 2010
My Family		Feb 2010
My Story		
My Friends		
Personalized Room Deco		Feb 2010
Mirror, Mirror		Feb 2010
Toy Barn		
Toy Bag		

Appendix B   Workshop Worksheet for Colors

	List Materials Assembled	Date Project Completed
Color Boxes		
Color Books		
Color Cards		*Mar 2010*
Color Crates		

Appendix C   Workshop Worksheet for Letters

	List Materials Assembled	Date Project Completed
Letter Cards		
Letter Toy Boxes		
Alphabet Boxes		
Letter Notebook		
Letter Pillows		
Magnetic Letters		May 2010
Alphabet Blocks		

Appendix D   Workshop Worksheet for Numbers

	List Materials Assembled	Date Project Completed
Number Books		
Sort o' Cards		
Counting Objects		
Dice		
Sponge Numbers		
Domino Number Cards		
Pick a Number		

Appendix E   Workshop Worksheet for Shapes

	List Materials Assembled	Date Project Completed
Shape Books		
Shape Boxes		
Shape Sorters		Jan 2010
Shape Collections		
Shape Seats		
Shape Sequences		

Appendix F   Workshop Worksheet for Reading

	List Materials Assembled	Date Project Completed
Word Books		
Word Notebook		
Categories Book		
Picture Cards		
Healthy Eating Cards		
Word Cards		
Word Puzzles		
Record a Book		

Appendix G   Record Sheet I

Activity	Sun.	Mon.	Tue.	Wed.	Thu.	Fri.	Sat.

Cognitive

Motor

Social

Language

Self-Confidence

Appendix H   Record Sheet II

Ideas	Sun.	Mon.	Tue.	Wed.	Thu.	Fri.	Sat.

Nutrition

Rest/Sleep

Self Help

Play

Miscellaneous

Parenting Information

Child-rearing ideas come to us from different directions. Some come directly from your own parents. They may offer specific tips such as "Read to your baby as soon as he is born." "Sing songs that you know and love to your baby." "Play lullabies at night." Other things you learned from them just because of the way they brought you up. Your childhood is actually the first stage of your parenting education. Your parents are always there to give you the benefit of their experience. If they were good models, you'll find it is easy to follow in their footsteps. If you suffered under their reign for any of many reasons, you may have a harder time parenting at first because you don't have wonderful examples to go by. But you will learn the ropes over time.

Complicating matters, times change! What worked for your parents may not work in the same way for you and your children, because the conditions you live with today are different than they were twenty or more years ago. No parenting advice is written in stone. The best advice instead captures the essence of good parenting, modified to fit current conditions.

Lots of good ideas and advice come from your friends. Other parents who are bringing up children will share helpful information with you, and strategies and techniques that worked for them. In addition to listening to what they say, look at what they do! Notice what works for them and what doesn't. It's natural to try out an idea with your own child that you saw worked for someone else and their child.

Computers offer website play, if you have access to the Internet. You can uncover your own favorite websites as you surf the web using key search words such as "child," "young children," "toddlers," "preschoolers," "play," and so on. Software created especially for children offers another option for computer play. There is much to choose from; any computer store can advise you on the wealth of programs available for young children and the particular software appropriate for the children aged one to three.

The Internet is becoming a wonderful source of parenting information. Website after website offers valuable parenting information you can use right away. Try these suggested sites:

www.fathers.com

For fathers, fathers-to-be, wannabe fathers, father figures, and fathers of fathers. The mission is to inspire and equip men to be better fathers.

www.parentpartners.com

For parents of children ages birth to five years. A comprehensive resource for child development information that combines knowledge of your child with the expertise of child-development specialists.

www.parentsoup.com

For mothers over thirty. This is the mother of parenting websites. It offers everything from daily news stories to emergency telephone numbers.

www.parenttime.com

For parents of children ages birth to six years. Owned by Time Inc. and Procter and Gamble, it publishes material by its staff and by the authors and editors of *Parenting* and *BabyTalk* magazines.

www.parenthoodweb.com

For parents of children ages birth to six years. It is well organized and substantive and includes a large section on pregnancy and labor.

www.parenting-qa.com

For parents of children ages birth to eighteen years. It answers questions pertaining to all aspects of parenting.

www.parents.com

For parents of children ages birth to eighteen years. A highly interactive site that draws from *Parents, Child, Family Circle,* and *McCall's* magazines.

www.parentsplace.com

For mothers over thirty. Has more than 400 bulletin boards and thousands of editorial pieces covering topics such as infertility, conception, pregnancy, complications, tests, childbirth, and postpartum care.

www.storksite.com

For parents of babies under one year of age. It specializes in pregnancy and raising infants.

www.abcparenting.com

For parents of children ages birth to six years. It functions as a directory and search engine for parents and parents-to-be.

www.babybag.com

For parents of children ages birth to five years. Has a helpful selection of tips and resources for parents, particularly in the areas of health and safety.

www.babycenter.com

For parents of babies under one year of age. Focuses on pregnancy through the first year. Also has a special area for dads, featuring fathers-only articles.

www.zerotothree.org

For parents and educators of children ages birth to three years. Provides information on growth and development for both parents and educators. Divided into two sections; the information is presented in ways that are appropriate for either group.

Taken from *Newsletter of the Center for the Improvement of Child Caring,* 2, no. 1, 1999.

In addition, look for a bonanza of parenting books and magazines in bookstores and libraries, and for parenting videos in video stores. Many schools have parenting resource centers with a variety of parenting materials. Child-care centers often provide parenting programs to educate parents on ways they can help their children. Special programs such as Early Head Start and Even Start help new parents who are in a low-income bracket. For those in need of special services because of difficult parenting situations, support programs like Children's Services Council, Healthy Mothers, Healthy Babies, Children's Home Society, and Child Development Services offer help. In addition, there are private "Mommy and Me" programs that provide play activities for parents and their young children and similar programs at centers such as the YWCA, churches, and temples. These organized programs often enrich their playtime with some parenting information as well.

Books. I heartily recommend *Your Baby & Child from Birth to Age Five* by Penelope Leach. The author is a pediatrician and an expert in all aspects of child care. Besides daily care, she will help you develop a stimulating educational and emotional environment for your child. You can make her your first stop before you call your doctor.

Magazines. Of the many that are available, several stand out:

- *Parents.* This popular magazine concentrates on information about children from birth to age thirteen. It offers advice on many family situations and challenges and covers topics including health and safety, time for you, family life, food, holiday celebrations, fun, and milestones of development.
- *Home Education.* With a focus on homeschooling, this magazine explains much about what it means to homeschool, describes different approaches, provides important legal information, suggests materials and resources, and puts you in touch with others who homeschool.

- *Mothering. Mothering* covers health issues, working directly with children, and issues related to pregnancy. The early years are emphasized.
- *Child.* It is a practical magazine about caring for children that emphasizes basics of health and safety, travel, nutrition, fashion, time for mom, and attention to special situations. Some general information about school-age children, but more information about infants, toddlers, and preschoolers.
- *Nick Jr.* This magazine for parents and preschoolers offers do-together games, booklets, and activities for preschoolers, and also simple pages that can be adapted for even younger children. A great source of pictures for many of the make-your-own toys in this book.

Videos. I particularly recommend a one-hour documentary called *Ten Things Every Child Needs,* which does an excellent job of explaining how parents' earliest interactions with children influence their development. The ten needs referred to by the title are interaction, loving touch, stable relationships, safe healthy environments, self-esteem, quality child care, play, communication, music, and reading. The host is television personality Tim Reid, with additional commentary by experts such as Dr. T. Berry Brazelton, Dr. Bruce Perry, and Dr. J. Felton Earls. WTTW Chicago and the Chicago Production Center produced this video for the Robert R. McCormick Tribune Foundation.

Stores. The Dollar Store is a popular place for inexpensive items that can be turned into simple toys. Other places to look are in large office supply stores, large drugstores, and even large grocery stores. Simple items combined with other simple items will make interesting toys about self-awareness, colors, letters, numbers, shapes, and reading.

Bibliography

American Natural Hygiene Society. *49 Tips for Maximizing Your Health—Naturally*. Tampa, Fla.: American Natural Hygiene Society, 2000.

Bloom. "Bloom on Books." *Cornell Alumni News* (September/October 2000), p. 55.

Bredekamp, S., ed. *Developmentally Appropriate Practices in Early Childhood Programs Serving Children from Birth Through Age 8*. Washington, D.C.: National Association for the Education of Young Children, 1998.

Carnegie Task Force on Meeting the Needs of Our Youngest Children. *Starting Points: Meeting the Needs of Our Youngest Children*. New York: Carnegie Corporation of New York, 1994.

Center for the Improvement of Child Caring. "Partners for Effective Parenting." *Newsletter of the Center for the Improvement of Child Caring* 2, no. 1, 1999.

Child: The Essential Guide for Parents, October 2000.

Granitur, E. *I Love You Daddy*. Miami Beach, Fla.: Sydney's Sproutin' Company, 1996a.

_____. *I Love You Daddy Even More*. Miami Beach, Fla.: Sydney's Sproutin' Company, 1996b.

_____. *We Love You Daddy*. Miami Beach, Fla.: Sydney's Sproutin' Company, 1996c.

Growing Child Publications, 22 North Second Street, P.O. Box 620, Lafayette, IN 47902–0620, 2000.

Hegener, Mark, and Helen Hegener. *Home Education* 17, no. 5, September–October 2000.

Leach, Penelope. *Your Baby and Child from Birth to Age Five*. New York: Alfred A. Knopf, 1998.

Maas, J. *Power Sleep*. New York: HarperPerennial, 1999.

Mothering Magazine. *Mothering: The Natural Family Living Magazine* 102 (September/October 2000).

Neufeldt, V., and A. N. Sparks. *Webster's New World Dictionary*. New York: Warner Books, Inc., 1990.

"Newsweek Special 2000 Edition: Your Child Birth to Three." *Newsweek* (Fall/Winter 2000).

Parents: America's #1 Family Magazine, October 2000.

Rick, S. *The Reflexology Workout*. New York: Crown Trade Paperbacks, 1986.

Robert R. McCormick Tribune Foundation. *Ten Things Every Child Needs*. Chicago: WTTW Chicago and the Chicago Production Center.

Schwartz, E., and Craig A. Conley. *Human Diversity: A Guide for Understanding*, 4th ed. New York: McGraw-Hill, 2000.

"Where Kids Play to Learn & Parents Learn to Play." *Nick Jr.* (October/November 2000).

White, B. L. *The First Three Years of Life*. New York: Fireside, 1998.

Index